Finding My Niche

A Memoir

Tim Woodward

Pediment Publishing, a division of The Pediment Group, Inc.,
Battle Ground, Washington 98604
www.pediment.com
© 2021 by Tim Woodward
All Rights Reserved. Published 2021.
Printed in the United States of America.

Library of Congress Control Number: 2021919079

ISBN: 978-1-59725-980-4

BOOKS BY TIM WOODWARD

Shirttail Journalist
McCracker Takes a Vacation
Here in Curmudgeons' Corner
Tiger on the Road: The Life of Vardis Fisher
Is Idaho in Iowa?
The Department of Yarns
Quintessential Boise (with Charles Hummel)
Destination Idaho
Finding My Niche

For My Children and Grandchildren

CONTENTS

PREFACE

The woman who edited my *Idaho Statesman* columns for a number of years emailed me one evening to say she had been laid off and that the email containing this news most likely would be my last from her.

Layoffs have been epidemic in the newspaper business. As of this writing, the number of employees at *The Statesman* is about ten percent of what it was at peak employment. Almost everyone I worked with there is gone. The editor ended her email by saying she hoped I could keep writing for the paper "for a while."

"A while," after more than forty years.

A while proved to be a little over a year. I wasn't laid off, but new newsroom management made it difficult for me to stay so I left for another newspaper. Despite a long run of mostly good fortune as a journalist, I had become vulnerable to the same fate that had befallen so many of my friends and former colleagues. Many were laid off after years or decades of devoted service. Others saw the future coming and gravitated to public relations or other fields as one newspaper after another ceased to exist. In an industry that once was one of the nation's largest employers, more than two thousand U.S. newspapers have shut down since 2004.

As a late friend was fond of saying, "nobody has a guarantee in their hip pocket that they'll be here tomorrow." It's time to write about my life—in and out of the newspaper business—before the tomorrows run out.

My adult life has been divided between journalism and music. It took four years of working other newsroom jobs to find my niche as a columnist. When I started playing in a band again after a twelve-year hiatus, the clash with my newspaper job was so disorienting that I wasn't sure which I was—a writer or a musician. It took a while to adjust to having two niches.

It's been said that to write a memoir you have to be famous or have done something extraordinary. Beyond a low-rent local celebrity, I have no claim to fame.

And though little of what I have done can be called extraordinary when compared with the feats of those who have distinguished themselves on a national or global stage, I do have a unique claim to having witnessed extraordinary growth and change in what was once a small, isolated town in an overlooked part of the country, and in a once powerful industry that has experienced a ruinous decline.

When I was growing up, Idaho was something of an obscurity to people in other parts of the country. More than once while killing time playing name-the-states-and-their-capitals during boring mid-watches in the Navy, fellow sailors would look at me incredulously and say, "You're from Idaho? That's the state we can't think of when we have the other forty-nine."

My growing-up years were a time of relative innocence. Boise then was about the size of Hobbs, New Mexico, today, and about as well known. Now it's one of the biggest cities in the Northwest and the Intermountain Region—larger than Tacoma, Spokane, or Salt Lake City—and in recent years has consistently been one of the fastest-growing cities in the nation.

We did not see this coming. I grew up in a town where there was no university, no football stadium with a famous blue field, no performing arts center, ballet company, or Shakespeare festival, no tall buildings, no traffic. For family entertainment, our parents drove my sister and me to a downtown railroad crossing in Dad's Buick to watch the trains come and go. My childhood friends and I played on vacant lots where homes have since grown old. We would not have believed what a difference a single lifetime could make.

I was a substitute paper boy when virtually every house on the route subscribed to *The Statesman*. Readers relied on it for everything: world, national, and local news; sports and society news, advertisements for everything from retail goods to movies to used cars. Its three daily editions were big and fat and profitable. *Statesman* editorial endorsements influenced elections. I started working there when newspapers were all but printing money and the newsroom pulsed with urgency and excitement.

As of this writing, the building that housed the state's largest newspaper for half a century is vacant, sold to a company that plans to convert it to storage units. The company that owns *The Statesman* has declared bankruptcy.

I witnessed these changes. I lived most of them. It's time to get them in down in print, before print itself becomes a memory.

— *Tim Woodward*

CHAPTER ONE
Family

O
n an otherwise ordinary morning of my sixteenth year, my mother paused as she headed for the door on her way to work and matter-of-factly said there was something she'd been meaning to discuss with me. She said it as if it were a trifle, like forgetting to make my bed or take out the trash.

I sat down on the living room couch, waiting to hear what she had to say.

It didn't take long.

"Do you know that your father and I both were married before we were married to each other?" she asked.

She might as well have asked if I'd known they were from a distant galaxy.

"Well, we were," she said, correctly interpreting my silence as a no.

"Remember the man who comes to the door with a present for Joanie every year at Christmastime?"

Joanie was my older sister.

"Yes, I remember him."

"Well, he's Joanie's father. That's why he always brings a present for her and not you. Daddy (the name she routinely used for my father) is your father. He's hers. Joanie isn't really your sister. She's your half sister."

I waited in silence, the power of speech having left me.

"Any questions?"

"Uh ... no."

"Good. I'm off to work," she said brightly. "See you tonight!"

It took a while—quite a while, actually—for the full impact of what she had revealed so offhandedly to sink in. My parents and my not-quite sister had been keeping a rather large secret from me my whole life. My mother had violated a tenet of the Catholic faith she held dear by divorcing her first husband, whose existence other than as a stranger at the door I'd never suspected. Divorce was all but forbidden by the Catholic Church in those days. What had he done that made her violate such a fundamental principle of her religion? And what had happened with my father's first marriage? Was his former wife still living? Did I have half sisters or brothers whose existence I never suspected?

I never learned the answers to most of those questions, and my parents weren't likely to have answered them except to provide bare-bones details. It was 1962. The openness that would characterize later times was unimaginable. Troubling facts that threatened the veneer of domestic tranquility were swept under the rug or, more likely in my mother's immaculate house, ionized by the Precipitron.

I didn't learn the answers at least partially because I didn't ask the questions, or spend time dwelling on them. Most kids couldn't care less about what their parents were before they were their parents. It only becomes important when they're older. Now, older, I resent my parents not telling me more and blame myself for not asking for more. Now that they're gone, I'd give a lot to have just an hour with them to fill in the gaps. My kids will probably do the same thing. They almost never ask me about my life prior to having them, let alone the lives of my parents or grandparents. They aren't interested, but they will be one day. They'll want to know more about their roots after I'm gone and it's too late.

My mother rarely spoke of her first husband. For all I know, he could have been a saint or a fiend. I was able to learn a little about him from her scrapbooks and public records, but my father's first wife is a complete mystery. He never once mentioned her to me, not even her name. If they had children, their identities and whereabouts also are a mystery.

Our parents' previous marriages explained why my sister and I were nothing alike, physically or otherwise. Neither of us bore the slightest resemblance to our mother, who in her early years had been stunning. A woman who knew her when both were teenagers remembered her as "someone you noticed. People paid attention whenever Marguerite O'Leary was around."

She inherited her good looks from her father's side of the family. William O'Leary Sr. grew up in Chicago. Mom and both of her brothers claimed to be descended from the O'Learys who were thought to have started the Great Chicago Fire of 1871 and which burned much of the city. Genealogical records show no direct connection between my mother's O'Learys and those blamed for the fire—wrongly, it now appears—but her heritage was evident in both her Irish temperament and her appearance.

As a young woman, she wore her auburn hair either swept up or in gentle waves, depending on the current fashion. In photos taken of her when she was in her twenties and thirties, she unfailingly was turned out in the latest styles. When the Beatles were popular, and I grew my hair out to look like theirs, she threatened to stop cooking my meals or washing my clothes until I got a haircut. She thought my long hair was a kind of rebellion. Told that it was the fashion, she relented. Fashion she understood.

Margaret O'Leary Woodward

Her eyes were blue, her complexion flawless. All her life, she took care to look her best, never dreaming of going out in public wearing anything she considered to be sloppy or in poor taste. Appearances—her own, her home's, her family's—were important to her. She must have told me a hundred times not to slouch, to stand up straight with my shoulders back, to look my best. It was crucial to make a good impression.

She was quick to laugh, even at herself. She had unshakable convictions, the Irish gift of gab and the Irish flair for colorful language.

"That's mighty thoughty of ya," she would say when someone did something nice for her.

She attempted to console my sister and me during troubled times by saying "you get used to hangin' if you hang long enough."

If someone insulted her, she didn't say it made her feel bad or that it hurt her feelings. It made her feel "like two cents waitin' for change."

It took gumption, in her view of the world, to get ahead in life. Gumption and "stick-to-it-iveness." I was not particularly motivated as a young boy. Truth be told, I was lazy, preferring to read, daydream, or lie around the house doing nothing to actually accomplishing anything. If I failed to do my chores or finish my homework, the expression I dreaded was quick in coming.

"You have to have stick-to-it-iveness, Tim," she would say. "You can't expect to amount to a hill of beans without it."

She married young, not long after a trip to California with a group of friends that included a young man named Ben Koppes, the soon-to-be father of my half sister. A scrapbook from the California trip is filled with photos of vibrant young people, my mother, and her friends. The men were handsome, the women knockouts. Beneath each photo are the names of the people pictured, white ink on black pages in my mother's lovely handwriting.

She talked about that trip for the rest of her life, saying it was the best time she ever had. She fell in love with Los Angeles, then about a fourth of its current population, wistfully recalling its balmy climate, fragrant orange groves, and boundless opportunities. She didn't want to come back to Idaho. She did—life isn't an orange grove—but she never completely stopped regretting it. She loved to sit in our darkened living room at night, smoking Pall Malls, and sharing memories. Often as not, on bleak winter evenings, they were memories of her California paradise lost.

My father, Bertram Francis Woodward, could not have been more different from my mother. He was born in Cripple Creek, Colorado, a mining town high in the Rockies, the son of a miner. Young Bert worked in the mines just long enough to know that he detested it. His father, Thomas Woodward, died of pneumoconiosis, a lung disease then commonly known as miner's consumption. Dad escaped his father's fate by running away from home as a teenager, returning to Cripple Creek only a few times during the rest of his life.

He didn't talk much about the hard times he faced after leaving home so young. He drifted, worked odd jobs. He worked briefly for an undertaker, claiming that he quit the night a corpse appeared to move and "frightened me out of a year's growth," and as a shoe salesman. He never did finish high school. Low-paying jobs and uncertainty of employment made him appreciate the importance of a good education, something he often stressed during my formative years.

We were having dinner in a Chinese restaurant the night I told him I might like to be a writer.

"The world is full of writers who are starving in the streets," he replied. "You need to do something practical. Do you think you might like to be a doctor or a lawyer?"

It was a recurring theme. He longed for his son to become a professional, to be spared the hardscrabble life he knew during his early years.

He had a temper. Angry about something long forgotten, he picked up a glass from his nightstand late one night and threw it against a wall, pieces of it shattering everywhere. I sometimes was afraid for him to come home from work when I was little, dreading a punishment for a transgression Mom judged to be serious enough to warrant the dreaded words, "wait till your father gets home." He was never abusive, but he didn't spare the rod when he thought it was deserved. The "rod" at our house was a sturdy Dutch Boy paint stick. I tried to burn it once, the unintended result being a paddling with a charred paint stick.

Bert Woodward

My temper may have come from Dad. Most people know me as easy going, but they don't see the anger, usually directed at myself for doing something stupid. Or at an inanimate object—a stubborn bolt, glasses that can't be found, a package that infuriatingly won't open. At such moments, I may look a little like Dad the night he threw the glass at the wall.

He had the strangest eating habits. His favorite delicacies included pickled pig's feet, soda crackers in buttermilk, and Jell-O drenched in sugar. So much sugar that the Jell-O itself wasn't visible. Even as a kid with a sweet tooth, it shocked me. I was in my early teens when he was diagnosed with diabetes. Medication and dietary changes wrought a miracle. Dad became a different man. His previously gray hair turned mostly dark again. His short temper vanished, never to return.

He was in his forties when he started a food brokerage business that was modestly successful. The basement and garage of my childhood home were stocked with samples of the products he peddled—Snowdrift shortening, Peter Pan peanut butter, Libby's canned goods, McDonald's candies, Portland Punch … His favorite dessert was vanilla ice cream topped with Portland Punch, a syrupy, berry-flavored concentrate now a memory. I was partial to the McDonald's candy and the pretty Peter Pan girls he used as models for displays in stores. He sold groceries to, among others, Joe Albertson, founder of the supermarket chain that bears his name. Dad was well liked and liked almost everyone. Except, for reasons he never explained, Joe Albertson.

And Howard Snyder, the neighborhood fix-it man who lived across the street. Howard was a big influence during my formative years. Though he never said so, Dad might have been a little jealous of that.

My sister married the boy next door. Literally. Joanie and David Robertson had two sons. After the birth of the second, she gained a lot of weight, enough that her husband left her. There may have been other reasons I never knew, but whatever the reasons she came home on a Thanksgiving Day, which also happened to be her birthday that year, to find him and everything he owned gone. She stayed in the house and cried for three days.

She lived in that house for the rest of her life, drove the same car for over twenty years, giving it up only when the cost of a major repair would have been more than the car was worth. She virtually never ventured outside of Boise, never changed her hairstyle or the way she dressed. It was as if she was permanently stuck in 1963.

All but one of my grandparents died before I was born. My maternal grandfather, William O'Leary, burned to death a month to the day before I was born. The stove he used to heat his home caught his house on fire while he slept. His wife, my grandmother Faye, had died of pneumonia years earlier. Except for a great-grandmother, the only grandparent I actually knew was my father's mother, Nell Woodward.

I was seven when the four of us—Mom, Dad, Joanie, and me—piled into

Dad's 1949 Buick for our one and only trip to Cripple Creek to visit her. Long widowed by then, she lived alone in a white, two-story house with a potbellied stove that glowed red-orange, taking the edge off of the mountain winters. She was a quiet woman who rarely spoke or smiled. My most vivid memory of her is of her repeatedly belching, unapologetically, at the dinner table. Most of Dad's relatives struck me as sober, humorless, and not particularly interesting in comparison with my mother's colorful Irish clan.

That applied with some degree of accuracy to Dad himself. He was a nice-looking man—good features, sky-blue eyes, hair combed straight back and never out of place. He could be and usually was pleasant. His smile was sincere and winning. But I cannot recall him telling a joke or a funny story, or laughing except on rare occasions. Perhaps because he worked so hard to escape a life of drudgery in the mines, he was a serious, hard-working man all his life. More often than not, our family vacations didn't include him because he had to work.

He had me doing household chores like shoveling coal and carrying out the clinkers from our coal-burning furnace when I was seven or eight. By age ten, I was in charge of mowing, weeding and the rest of the yard work. I was mortified when, to the surprise of everyone including the lifeguards, Dad bypassed the pay desk, threaded his way through the boys' changing room and appeared fully clothed in slacks and a dress shirt on the edge of our neighborhood's municipal swimming pool to drag me home because I hadn't mowed the lawn.

By the time I was thirteen, he reasoned that I was old enough to work for the company that he and one of my uncles had started a few years earlier, installing lawn-sprinkling systems. (Evergreen Sprinkler Company, founded in 1957, exists to this day.) It was hot, hard work, most of it on the end of a shovel, nine hours a day, six days a week. The pay, unchanged for the four summers I worked there, was a dollar an hour.

Though he didn't finish high school, Dad was well educated in the school of life. He read widely and was an excellent businessman. Guilty of an occasional grammatical error in causal speech, he went out of his way to assure that the grammar and spelling in his business letters were perfect. As a salesman, he was a marvel. He never pressured his customers. His low-key approach and straight answers to their questions made them sense that they could trust him. Looking for something to keep him busy after he and my uncle sold the sprinkler business, he went to work selling real estate signs for a company based in Kansas. Then in his eighties and competing against much younger men, he became its top salesman.

From my father I learned to work hard, be responsible and always tell the truth. He was the most honest man I've ever known. One day in a supermarket, perhaps as an example for yours truly, he picked up a dime on the floor and turned it in as lost property.

From my mother I learned to appreciate life, enjoy what it had to offer and laugh at its twists and turns. It was from her side of the family that I inherited a love of music and a good story. She used to sit in the living room and listen to my Beatles albums on the stereo, commenting on songs she thought were beautiful and asking me to play them for her again. She wasn't an avid reader, but she could tell a story with the best of them. And she taught me the value of laughing at life's curveballs. When the radiator of her Nash Rambler erupted with a fountain that rivaled Old Faithful during a vacation trip to Yellowstone Park, she laughed at the geyser of steaming water and at our predicament. Soon she had me and my sister laughing, too. This would pass. And the spectacle of the three of us gathered round her custom-painted, chartreuse and black Nash Rambler in the middle of a desert wasn't without an element of comedy. She made us laugh when many would have cursed.

On another of our trips (Dad again stayed home), we drove the Rambler to California to visit her brother Bill and his wife, Mary, who lived in Los Altos. Her other brother, Allen, drove Mom, Joanie, and me from Los Altos to Disneyland during our California odyssey. We made the trip, a distance of some 400 miles, in his Plymouth Valiant, which rivaled the Ford Edsel as one of the ugliest automobiles ever built. Except for Uncle Allen, who lived in Oakland, none of us had ever seen a freeway before. We'd heard stories about California's freeways, but this was our first encounter with one.

We were coming into Los Angeles at an alarming rate of speed in heavy traffic, Uncle Allen's knuckles white on the wheel, when we passed an ancient truck with what appeared to be all of its owners' earthly possessions piled high in the back and secured with ropes. It could have been a scene from *The Grapes of Wrath*. The driver, his wife, and their children looked terrified. As we were about to pass them, one of the ropes came loose and everything went flying. Boxes and suitcases opened midair, their contents spilling onto the freeway. Clothes, towels, sheets, and blankets, books, chairs, everything but a few heavy items of furniture were scattered across multiple lanes. That no one crashed trying to miss them was a minor miracle. It was terrible for that poor family, but at age twelve I thought it was just about the funniest thing I'd ever seen.

Uncle Allen went off the grid not long after that. Up until then he'd sent us a wooden crate at Christmastime, filled with gifts and a rare treat of fragrant California oranges. Oranges weren't sold in Boise in the winter in those days. One year the crates stopped coming, as did his letters. My mother fretted, ultimately resigning herself to the possibility that her brother had died alone in California with no one to notify his relatives in Idaho. After several years without a word, a letter arrived. He casually apologized for not writing sooner, as if it had been weeks rather than years. His letters continued sporadically for a couple of years before trailing off again.

Years later, grown and on assignment in the Bay Area as a journalist, I went to the Oakland return address on one of Mom's old letters. It was an apartment building in a not-so-great neighborhood. Climbing a set of stairs to the apartment number on the address, I knocked on the door and waited, expecting to be told that Allen O'Leary had long since died or moved away.

But there he was! Older, obviously, but I recognized his kindly Irish face immediately. It was mid-afternoon, but he was dressed in pajamas and a robe. He was barefoot, and several of his toes had been amputated. Initially he was wary, not believing I was who I claimed to be. Only after mentioning the oranges he used to send at Christmas and the family's belongings flying off of their truck on our trip to Disneyland did he relax a bit. We reminisced for a while, but it was awkward. He clearly was uncomfortable with having a visitor, never opening the door more than a few inches. Heat boiled from his apartment as if from a blast furnace. With the small talk over, nothing was left to say. I thanked him for his time and wished him well. He died not long afterwards.

His brother, Bill, was smart, charismatic, and slightly to the right of Genghis Khan. A member of the John Birch Society and other ultraconservative organizations, he believed the country was in danger of being taken over by the Communists at any moment. In addition to being terrified of Communists, he and his wife, my Aunt Mary, were convinced that the end of the world was imminent. It was one prophesy of doom after another with them.

The most memorable was the Chastisement. The Chastisement, as they explained it, would be something like the time in ancient Egypt when Jews were warned to mark their doors with lamb's blood during Passover to spare their firstborn from a plague. Nothing would do but for our entire extended family to shelter in a safe place, with newspapers taped over the windows, in theory to protect us against the imminent horror. The place chosen to hunker down was Joanie's house. With the doors locked and the windows duly covered, we nervously went to bed.

Early the next morning—it was still dark—my wife and I awoke to the sound of ghostly music. Until then, we had been skeptical. The music changed that.

"Do you hear that?"

"Yes, what is it?"

"Listen! They were right, after all! This is it!"

It wasn't. It was the radio on Joanie's radio alarm clock, playing the psychedelic introduction to a song. When the day dawned normally and passed without incident, Uncle Bill and Aunt Mary were not in the least sheepish about having conned us all into hiding behind newspapered windows (they saw mainstream newspapers as instruments of Communist propaganda, incidentally), quaking over an apocalyptic scenario that never happened. Neither of them ever mentioned the Chastisement again, a pattern repeated multiple times through the years with other doomsday scenarios that proved to be utter nonsense.

All of the O'Learys, along with my father and mother, were devout Catholics—old-school, pre-Vatican II Catholics. My parents would no more have questioned or disobeyed a church pronouncement than they would have cheated on their taxes or joined a motorcycle gang. Their unwavering adherence to church doctrine explained why they slept in separate bedrooms. The church had declared the dissolution of their previous marriages sufficient reason to consign them to a marriage without intimacy, a life outside looking in through the church's stained-glass windows. They were allowed to attend Mass, which they did faithfully every Sunday, but not to receive communion. It had to have haunted them, but they never rebelled or questioned it. All their lives, they cherished and clung to the traditional Catholicism they revered despite its effect on their marriage.

If their decision to keep the fact of their former marriages from their son until he was nearly grown seems overly protective or even bizarre by today's standards, allowances must be made for the fact that society was different then. Divorce was less accepted, almost a stigma, and my parents were nothing if not representative of their time and place. Parents so sheltered their kids that few of us growing up in Boise of the 1950s had any idea that the Boys of Boise scandal, which was making national headlines, existed. No one, at least in the presence of children, uttered the words "homosexual" or "pedophile." We were warned to avoid a certain shop whose offerings otherwise would have made it a magnet for young boys because its owner was not to be trusted. Why he wasn't to be trusted was never specified. We knew only that it involved something dark and sinister, which we would understand when we were older.

Boise, like much of the Northwest in those days, was almost exclusively white. There were so few people of color that the average white person could and routinely did go weeks without seeing one. Most of the city's Black people lived in a neighborhood that many whites referred to with a blatantly racist name. We were so ignorant of what life was like for minorities that not until the Civil Rights Movement did it occur to us how despicable such expressions were. It wasn't until my first year of high school that I actually knew a Black person. He was instantly likable, a popular student at our school and an antidote to the casual prejudice we grew up with in our white world.

Our world was isolated, insulated—a geographic and cultural island. Boise's population seemed permanently stuck at about 35,000. Cosmopolitan cities like Seattle and Denver were hundreds of miles away. This meant, among other things, that there wasn't much in the way of urban amenities. Change, when it came at all, came slowly. Music, art, and fashions, even chain stores and restaurants that were common in other places, didn't reach us until they were old news everywhere else. We had two television channels and two airlines, United and West Coast. An oft-told tale had it that an airline pilot on approach to our modest airport made the following announcement:

"Ladies and gentlemen, we're about to land in Boise, Idaho. Please set your watches back twenty years."

An exaggeration, but not by much. Boise was, to a significant degree, a provincial, locally owned outpost. The power and water companies and other utilities all were locally owned. All five of the theaters and three of the five department stores were locally owned. C. C. Anderson's namesake owner roamed the aisles of his store like Santa Claus in a business suit, his pockets filled with candy for youthful customers. The most upscale department store was the Mode, Ltd. It had high-end products with prices to match, a tea room, and a patrician owner known to most simply as

"Mrs. Chapman." The low-end store was the Cash Bazaar, also owned and operated by a local family. All but a few of the shops and restaurants were local. Eateries from drive-ins to fine dining establishments were owned by local people rather than distant corporations. There were no McDonalds, Burger Kings, or Taco Times, no Red Robins, P. F. Chang's, or Tony Roma's. Even the newspaper, *The Idaho Daily Statesman*, was owned by a local woman, Margaret Cobb Ailshie. She inherited it from her father, Calvin Cobb.

My earliest memory of the local paper is of the pastor of our church, Father John Creegan, saying—from the pulpit—that "that damned *Statesman* can't get anything right." The reason for so uncharacteristic an outburst was that the paper had printed incorrect information about the Saint Mary's Ball, the parish's social and fundraising event of the year.

Though yet to have much interest in the news, I seldom missed a *Statesman* story about the local minor league baseball team, our beloved Boise Braves, and I felt like someone punched me when the *Statesman* carried a story about the death of John Steinbeck, my literary hero and the reason I wanted to become a writer. My introduction to politics came in *Statesman* stories about U.S. Senator Frank Church, who had visited our neighborhood while campaigning. Later, as a young teen, I followed the presidential campaign of the youthful John F. Kennedy, the young people's candidate, in the *Statesman*. Dad and Uncle Wayne advertised their sprinkler business in the *Statesman*. My mother enjoyed reading and drolly commenting on the society news at a time when newspapers published everything from prominent people's travel itineraries to the guest lists of parties they hosted. People clipped and saved stories about friends' and family members' engagements, weddings, and anniversaries. Readers perused *The Statesman*'s classified advertisements for automobiles, used furniture, musical instruments, jobs, bicycles, pets … It was a force in everyday life.

Mom, never at a loss for a colorful expression, had her own name for *The Statesman*. Over breakfast and her morning coffee, she would open the newspaper, smile good-naturally, and say, "Let's see what's in The Daily Blab today."

I was an unshakable optimist then. There wasn't the slightest doubt that I would be the next John Steinbeck. Or, in the off chance that that didn't happen, a dashing Pan American World Airways pilot. My interest in The Daily Blab was limited to the few subjects that personally interested me. Never in my youthful imaginings did it occur to me that I would spend most of my working life there.

CHAPTER TWO
A Good Place to Grow Up

I was born on a windy October evening at Boise's old Saint Alphonsus Hospital, a turreted Queen Anne-style building presided over by black-robed nuns. My mother recalled that she and my father sat outside in the car for a while, trying to decide whether the labor pains were real or a false alarm. I can imagine their faces: Dad, worried; Mom, smiling and telling him to relax.

My father wanted to name me Winfield, after a boyhood friend. I'd have given a lot to have heard their conversation when he dropped that alliterative bomb.

"You want to name our son *Winfield Woodward?*"

"Yes, I thought a lot of my friend Winfield, and I think it would be a nice name for him."

"*Winfield?* You think Winfield would be a nice name when most boys his age have names like Jim or John or Tom or Bob?"

"We could call him Win for short."

"*Win Woodward?* That's as bad if not worse!"

My mother prevailed, thank God, and I went home from the hospital as Timothy Joseph. Tim wouldn't have been my choice for a name, but we don't get to name ourselves and there was no denying that it beat Winfield.

Their home at the time was a basement apartment that I remember absolutely nothing about it because the family moved in my infancy to what was wincingly referred to for years to come as "the blue house." Judging by my parents' and sister's recollections of it, a more appropriate color would have been lemon yellow. They grimaced and shook their heads when recalling its deficiencies—leaky plumbing, poor insulation, a fireplace that nearly burned the house down. ... They were there months rather than years before moving to the first home I do remember, on Nineteenth Street in Boise's North End.

It was an old, creaky, two-story house—dark, dreary, dilapidated. I remember only two of the neighbors. Mrs. McMurren lived next door and occasionally babysat me. She was a kindly, elderly woman who made delicious soup that helped compensate for missing my mother during her infrequent absences. Our other next-door neighbors had a boy named Scotty, a year or so older than me and a bully.

It was Scotty who decided to give me a haircut one day and scissored off part of the scalp on the back of my head. A scar still marks the spot. He enjoyed pounding on me for sport as well. My mother complained to his mother, with little effect. This continued until the day I took matters into my own hands.

I was too much younger and smaller than Scotty to take him on in a fight, but a chance for revenge came in the form of a deep trench a plumber had dug in our front yard to repair a leak. With Scotty standing at the edge of the trench curiously peering down, it was clear that the moment had come. Quiet as a church mouse, I tiptoed up behind him and pushed him in. His wails could be heard up and down the block and were a source of almost unbearable pleasure. His mother presently rescued him, then tore into my mother about what a monster she was raising. Mom calmly but firmly reminded her about all the times her monster had sent me home bleeding from their house. After they left, she said she was proud of me for sticking up for myself but not to push anyone into a ditch ever again.

This was the first of several incidents during my youth that would raise the ire of neighborhood mothers.

Most of my memories of Nineteenth Street are small, insignificant ones. Amos and Andy and Molly and Fibber McGee on the radio, begging my mother for spoonfuls of sweet, syrupy Vi-Daylin vitamins, the night the bat got in. My mother and sister, armed with brooms, ran about shrieking and waving the brooms in hopes of vanquishing it. That kind of excitement happened rarely at our house. I enjoyed it immensely.

My most vivid memory of Nineteenth Street is of Thanksgiving dinner the year I turned four. Mom had invited my great-grandmother Susie and her last husband, whom I knew only as Grandpa Chandler. My mother worshiped Grandma Susie, with good reason. She had crossed the plains in a covered wagon, lost everything in three house fires, and had lost two husbands and three of her four children. Yet she remained a positive, jovial soul, loved by all. She worked for many years as a cook at a veterans' residence known as "The Old Soldiers' Home," now the site of a state park dedicated to veterans.

Grandpa Chandler, her third husband, was a nice old man who dressed in three-piece suits when they came to visit and always had a pocketful of pennies for me. We were having dinner that Thanksgiving when he slumped over at the table. My father and an uncle carried him to an upstairs bedroom while my mother called for help. It wasn't long afterwards that grim-faced ambulance attendants carried him out on a stretcher. It was the last time we ever saw him. Grandma Susie seemed to take it in stride. She'd suffered so many losses, and was nothing if not resilient.

Nineteenth Street was a temporary home, a place to live while my folks saved money to build their dream house. In June 1951, we moved to their new home in an area of North Boise that in those days was still being developed. Today the North End is a trendy, established neighborhood of older homes, with some of the highest residential real estate prices in Idaho. The one my folks built for $13,000, a formidable sum for them at the time, was valued at the time of this writing at more than $600,000.

To them, it was more than a house. Memories of the Great Depression and World War II were fading as the nation entered a new era of prosperity. We and our new neighbors were among the beneficiaries, living in modest but comfortable homes in a good neighborhood. It was my parents' payoff for years of hard work during hard times. They had lived through the 1918 Flu Pandemic, the Great Depression, and World War II, during which Dad served in the Marine Corps. Mom and Dad were a traveling sales team early in their marriage. She previously had worked as a clerk in a Boise department store—they met when she sold him a gift for his mother—and her sales skills were put to use on the road. He sold groceries; she sold jewelry. They survived treacherous mountain passes, howling storms, broken-down cars, and rundown hotels in nowhere towns in Idaho, Oregon, Washington, Wyoming, and Montana. With the war over and the road behind them, they could concentrate on raising a family in their newly completed home, on the corner of Twenty-Fifth and Lemp Streets, at the dawn of the peaceful, prosperous 1950s.

The house was modest by today's standards—two bedrooms, one bathroom, an attached, one-car garage, a recreation room, laundry room, and furnace room in the basement. Compared with the drafty, bat-infested house that preceded it, however, it was a showplace. My mother poured her heart and energies into choosing the paint and wallpaper, carpets, draperies … everything. The living room was resplendent in dark green wallpaper with pine cones. The drapes were bright red with bold slashes in black and white. The kitchen was a cheerful yellow and sported my mother's pride and joy—a built-in China closet. Everything was new and gleaming and modern in ways that all but screamed 1950s. Ward and June Cleaver would have felt right at home there.

Kids today wouldn't know what to make of everyday household items widely used then. Contemporary teenagers proficient in every aspect of digital technology would be undone by the clunky, rotary-dial telephones of the era. Spinning a dial to make a call or calling a number to get the correct time or directory assistance would have been alien concepts to them. My job of filling the coal hopper and carrying out the clinkers they'd deem prehistoric, as they would my mother's wringer washer and back-yard clothesline. We had a phonograph that played the likes of Rodgers and Hammerstein on 78 rpm records. There was no television for the first several years at our new house. Boise had two television channels in those days. Local kids' programming consisted of Sheriff Spud on Channel Seven and the Merry Milkman on Channel Two.

Twist-top lids were a new, initially baffling innovation. My mother was reduced almost to the point of swearing, which she almost never did, by her inability to open a jelly jar with a hand-held can opener. She almost destroyed the lid trying to pry it loose.

"All you have to do is twist the lid," one of my youthful friends told her.

It was her first encounter with a twist-top lid that didn't have to be pried open. Looking first at my friend, then at the mangled lid, she twisted it off and laughed. Angry as she'd been at the recalcitrant lid, a five-year-old telling her how to open a jar of jelly tickled her funny bone.

Our dream house had one bathtub, and for many years no shower. My mother washed my hair in the kitchen sink, where we also washed and dried dishes. No dishwasher.

No air conditioning, either. On summer days so hot that the tar streets bubbled in the sun, we kept all the blinds in the house closed during the heat of the day. At night, we turned box fans to high and opened all the windows to let in the cooler night air. In the winter, we slept in flannel pajamas under heavy wool blankets and quilts with hot water bottles at the bottom of the bed to keep our feet warm. On rainy or snowy days, we wore galoshes to play or go to school. My father's term for galoshes was "rubbers" (to my later embarrassment and endless teasing from the boys who would become my teenage friends).

Tim, sitting on wagon; Timmy Hally standing. The picture was taken in front of Tim's parents' house on Lemp Street in Boise's North End. The street was a dirt road then. Now one of Boise's oldest and priciest neighborhoods, the North End still had vacant lots in those days.

Once every week, at noon, an air raid sounded. Heard all over town, it was regularly tested to make sure everyone knew what to do in case the Reds decided to push the button down. Dad toyed with the idea of having a bomb shelter built in our back yard.

Boise of the 1950s was in most ways a great place to grow up. Kids lived a Huckleberry Finn–type of existence, free to explore the city at will, roaming its length and breadth on foot or on bicycles in search of fishing holes, tadpole ponds, and other attractions. The only rule: be home for dinner.

One of earliest memories of life at our new house is of sitting on the curb in front of the house playing with rocks in the gutter—kids didn't have as many diversions in those days—when a boy my age walked up and sat down beside me. We were both a few months short of five.

This was a new experience. There hadn't been any boys close to my age on Nineteenth Street except for Scotty, who hardly qualified as a friend. Indeed the very concept of friendship was uncharted territory. The boy's name was Tim Hally. We played with the rocks for a while and agreed to meet later. Timmy—people called me Tim and him Timmy to avoid confusion—was my first friend in the neighborhood, my first friend ever.

Others soon followed. Bill Molitor, who lived a block away and was exactly three weeks older than me, was next. That same summer, a family from Utah, the Baders, moved into the big, two-story house catty-corner from ours. Their son, also our age, was named Billy. In the course of a summer, the neighborhood went from having no pre-school age boys to having four. We remained friends until high school, when childhood friendships tend to fade. The Baders eventually moved away, but Tim Hally, Bill Molitor, and I remained, if not close friends, at least on friendly terms for life.

That there were no televisions in our pre-school years was probably a blessing. As our parents never tired of reminding us, we had to make our own fun. This sometimes ended badly, particularly when it came to my exploits involving Timmy Hally.

The Hallys lived two houses away from ours. Timmy was the youngest of four boys. Their father was an engineer. He helped design one of Idaho's iconic bridges and had attended Gonzaga University with Bing Crosby, destined for fame as a singer and actor. A picture of Crosby and Mr. Hally together in their college days graced the family's living room. Mr. Hally drove a sumptuous, black Buick Roadmaster with a back-seat armrest that doubled as a hiding place for a bottle of whisky. Mrs. Hally was an avid Democrat who worked tirelessly in behalf of Frank Church, who went on to serve three terms in the Senate and chair the Senate Foreign Relations Committee. The Hallys were a family with whom you wanted to be on good terms. When it came to my misadventures with their youngest son, the terms couldn't have been much worse.

The first mishap occurred in their basement, where the floor tiles formed a shuffleboard-court pattern. Timmy and I were playing there one day when he did something, now forgotten, that annoyed me enough to throw one of the shuffleboards at him. I didn't mean to hurt him, but the shuffleboard hit him squarely in the mouth with enough force that he bled profusely. Fearing his front teeth had been knocked out, I ran home and told my mother, who returned with me in tow to the scene of the crime. Mrs. Hally was standing over her son at the bathroom wash basin, wiping his mouth with a wash cloth. I'll never forget her words:

"I don't want you playing with that Woodward kid any more. I can't wait to get my hands on that goon."

She didn't realize that the goon and his mortified mother were standing inches behind her.

The embarrassment the remark caused may have been a factor in her eventual change of heart. It wasn't long before Timmy was allowed to consort with the goon again, often to his peril.

The oddest things used to turn up in North End alleys. One looked for all the world like a torpedo, several feet long and shaped exactly like a torpedo, fins and all. I have no idea what it actually was, but I happily dragged it home, hardly believing my good fortune in finding such a treasure. My mother, fearing that it was an undetonated explosive of some sort, grounded me. My memories of World War II were nonexistent. Hers were fresh.

Another alley oddment remains inexplicable to this day. It was a baton with a concrete sphere roughly the size of softball attached to one end. Why or how anyone would turn a baton into a lethal weapon was a mystery, but it made a highly entertaining toy. I took it home and pretended to vanquish make-believe bad guys by bonking them over the head with it. It was a harmless pastime—until I pretended to bonk a bad guy who was walking out the back door of our garage at the precise instant that the hapless Hally exited the door. He wasn't unconscious for very long, but weeks passed before he was allowed to expose himself to further pain and suffering at the Woodward residence.

Not enough weeks, apparently. Poor Timmy walked out of the same garage door on another day later that summer—I had no idea he was anywhere around—just as I released an arrow aimed at a target nailed to a fence. It didn't exactly stick in his ribs, but it tore a hole in his shirt and bled enough to result in another suspension from playing with the neighborhood troublemaker.

Mrs. Hally, if you're reading this in the next life, it was an accident. Honest, Mrs. Hally—they were all accidents! I never intended to harm, maim or kill your son.

Misadventures notwithstanding, life was peaceful in the old neighborhood most of the time. The nearby kid magnets were conveniently located within a block of each other, and a mere three-block walk from home. Lowell Grocery, at the corner of Twenty-Eighth and Heron Streets, was well-stocked with all sorts of treasures. Across the street, Lowell School boasted one of the city's biggest playgrounds. Just north of the school was Lowell Municipal Swimming Pool.

Lowell Grocery sold suckers, candy cigarettes, Jaw Breakers, Lik-M-Aid, and other treats for a penny apiece. For those who wanted to spend a whole nickel,

there were chocolate bars, Sidewalk Sundaes, Black Cows, Switzer's licorice bars …
A block away, at Twenty-Eighth and Lemp, a new M&W Store had a bakery with
mouth-watering pastries from Splendid Bakery, run by a neighbor, Ray Hohenleitner,
who conveniently lived a block away. The store also had a machine filled with
glistening bottles of soda pop—Nehi, Grapette, R.C. Cola, Dad's Root Beer, and
others—suspended in ice from metal slats that held the bottles by their rims. You
put a nickel in a slot and a mechanism opened, allowing you to slide a bottle from
the slats and lift it from the ice water. The first time I recall being outraged was when
the price doubled from a nickel to a dime. If President Eisenhower had intervened,
inflation could have been stopped then and there.

The toy offerings at Lowell Grocery included two of our summer mainstays:
slingshots and pea shooters. These simple toys brought hours of entertainment for
the neighborhood kids and ongoing frustration for their parents.

Slingshots could be dangerous. A rock fired from one could put out an eye. We
instinctively knew this and favored targets tacked to fences over shooting at each
other. Vastly preferable to rocks were little white balls filled with white powder.
Purchased for a few cents at Lowell Grocery, they exploded on impact, leaving a
white circle on whatever they hit. This could be anything from a fence to a telephone
pole to the side of a house. The neighborhood grownups understandably weren't
crazy about them.

Pea shooters, for those unfamiliar with them, were plastic straws big enough
for a pea or a bean to be fired through them with a mouthful of air and durable
enough to last most of a summer. For a reason lost in time, we shot beans rather
than peas with our pea shooters. Bean wars were a favorite summer pastime. There
was something enormously satisfying about putting a Navy bean in your mouth and
expelling it through the straw with sufficient force to propel it fifteen or twenty feet,
ideally striking a target that could be anything from a stop sign to another kid. By
the time the summer ended or we had moved on to other pastimes, we collectively
had fired hundreds if not thousands of beans at various objects and one another.

Short of a direct hit in an eye, which I don't recall happening, there was little
chance of anyone's being hurt. What drove the parents wild wasn't the risk of injury,
but the aftermath of bean mania. By late summer, every lawn in the neighborhood
had sprouted scores of bean plants. We thought it was funny; Jack and the Beanstalk
on steroids. Our parents did not see the humor. My folks were meticulous about

maintaining their house and yard. When a few errant leaves blew onto the lawn from a neighbor's yard after ours had been raked, out came the rakes again, accompanied by inordinate grumbling. So it wasn't surprising that their reaction to bean plants coming up every few feet in their manicured lawn was just short of apoplectic. My suggestion, that they stop mowing for a while and harvest the beans, was not well received.

Contemporary parents would be horrified if their children engaged in activities we routinely enjoyed. Dirt-clod fights, for instance. The neighborhood's vacant lots were a reliable source of dirt clods ideal for throwing. Sides were chosen, clods were gathered and the battles commenced. We were lucky no one was seriously injured.

Not all of our pastimes were risky or causes of parental concern. When I was maybe five or six, one of the neighbor's dogs had puppies that they were giving away. Succumbing to relentless pleading, Mom and Dad agreed to let me take one home. He was small and black and cuddly. I named him Champ. Within minutes of taking him home, I was sneezing and scratching my eyes. This was followed by mild asthmatic symptoms, convincing my folks that Champ had to go. To overcome my resistance, they resorted to bribery. If I agreed to take Champ back to his original owners, they would buy me a set of switches for my electric train.

It was an effective strategy. Like every other boy in the neighborhood, I was bewitched by model railroads. It was sad to lose Champ, but nice not to be feeling like a candidate for an antihistamine commercial. And playing with a train that could be switched from one stretch of tracks to another was a beautiful thing. Mine was a Lionel train with a heavy, metal locomotive, unlike the lightweight plastic ones made today, and a string of box cars. Dad set it up on a ping pong table in the basement. It was at its best at night, with the lights turned off, the room illuminated only by the locomotive's headlight and the red and green lights of the crossing signals. Playing with the train was for the most part a solitary pastime, one I enjoyed as much as playing outdoors with friends. I spent untold hours in the darkened basement, lovingly fingering the transformer levers and pressing the buttons for the switches, watching the lights cut the blackness, mesmerized.

Boys and girls alike spent hours playing marbles in the alley behind my parents' house. The usual game involved drawing a circle in the sandy dirt, arranging marbles inside it and from the edge of the circle shooting marbles at the ones inside the circle. If you knocked an opponent's marble out of the circle in a game of "keepsies," it was yours. Some of the marbles were ball bearings, or "steelies." "Clearies" were glass marbles of one color and no patterns or designs. "Cat's eyes" were clear marbles with a swirl of color in the middle. Others were opaque with a variety of colors and designs. Marbles roughly twice as large as the others were "boulders." I kept my marbles in a velvet bag with a drawstring, polished them lovingly and wrapped the clearies, my favorites, with aluminum foil. It stung to lose a cleary to an opponent.

Frog races were another way of passing summer days. At the northern edge of town was a hill called Camel's Back, for its shape, and behind the hill was a pond teeming with tadpoles. We'd ride our bikes to the hill, climb over it to the other side and catch tadpoles in Mason jars. At home, the tadpoles were transferred to goldfish bowls, where, with agonizing slowness, they sprouted legs, dropped their tails and became frogs.

Every kid in the neighborhood had at least one frog to place on a starting line and cheer for in the races, the outcomes of which were seldom clear. Unlike horses on a track, frogs go pretty much wherever they please. Still, it was a pleasant way to spend a lazy summer afternoon. The frogs weren't harmed and didn't seem to mind. It was a night-and-day different world then. If I suggested catching tadpoles or racing frogs to my grandchildren, they'd look at me as if I had frogs growing out of my nostrils.

The biggest single event for the neighborhood children during my growing-up years, without a close second, was the construction and opening of Lowell Municipal Pool in the summer of 1953. Most of the neighborhood kids would have been seven or eight then, and we were delirious with excitement. Never mind that none of us could swim a stroke. We knew all too well that any day it would be full summer, when temperatures soared to 100 degrees or more. Now we would have relief. We would have a pool. We would learn to swim.

After a few rudimentary lessons from the pool's instructors, we were ready to go. At least we thought so. By the time the summer heated up in mid-June, we were doing cannonballs and daring each other to ascend the ladder to the high dive and plunge into the deep end. Alarmed upon learning this, our mothers rose up, insisting en masse that we take proper swimming lessons at the YMCA. When we were promoted from tadpoles to flying fish at the first lesson, they relented, stopped making us go to the Y, and the rest of the summer was ours to enjoy the new municipal pool without restrictions.

Its design was unusual in that it wasn't at ground level. You entered through double doors, paid an admission fee at the front desk and, after passing through a changing room with showers and dressing cubicles, climbed concrete stairs to the pool itself, a circle of sparkling blue. I can see it now, smell the chlorine, hear the slap-slap-slap of flip flops on wet pavement. The pool was a regular hangout for most of every summer for several years. My pals and I alternated between swimming and flirting with the lifeguards, who were older and considered us obnoxious pests.

Unable to wait for the pool's official opening one year, Bill Molitor and I scaled the wall and sneaked in in hopes of getting a head start on the summer. We had the pool all to ourselves on a moonlit May night. If the water hadn't been cold enough to turn our fingernails blue, we probably would have done it repeatedly and gotten caught.

Across the street from the pool, Hamburger Korner (spelled with a 'k' to give it some class), did a brisk business in burgers, fries, shakes, malts, and flavored Cokes. The house specialty was the Belly Buster, a double burger with a slice of ham and "special sauce." A guilty pleasure in today's world, but in those days an innocent taste of heaven.

Timmy Hally and I and a neighbor girl, Joanne Robertson, were pedaling home from Hamburger Korner one afternoon when I hopped off of my bicycle partway home and one of the handlebars hit me just above my right eye. The rubber grip on that end of the handlebar was missing, and its sharp metal edge cut a gash in my forehead. It took about five seconds to realize how much head wounds can bleed. By the time Timmy and Joanne walked me home, my swimsuit and the right side of my body from my face down to my flip flops were bloody.

Joanne rang the doorbell, and we waited on the front porch. My mother answered the door, perhaps expecting a delivery or a visit from of the neighbors. She took one look and fainted.

When we weren't swimming, we were likely to be playing baseball. Boys breathed baseball in the 1950s, before football skyrocketed in popularity and baseball truly was the national pastime. My father and I played catch in the back yard and listened to minor league games on the radio of his Buick over root beer floats at the Frostop drive-in. My baseball-smitten friends and I traded baseball cards. We attended games at Braves Field, where our beloved Boise Braves played the Salt Lake City Bees, Great Falls Electrics, Magic Valley Cowboys, and other Pioneer League teams.

We spent hours oiling our gloves to supple perfection with Three-in-One Oil. But mostly, we played baseball.

We'd arrive at Lowell School, which had the biggest playground for miles, early enough in the morning that the field was still wet with dew. Play typically began with leaning our bikes against the backstop, choosing teams, and arguing about who would play what position and which team would bat first. The argument was a tradition. The game couldn't begin without it.

With the first hit, the ball cracked from the bat and flung droplets of water as it scudded across the field, leaving a dark trail in the silver-wet grass. On the next hit, the sound wouldn't be as crisp when the ball left the bat. The ball gradually became waterlogged, the crack a heavy thud. We didn't care. We played until the ball dried. We played for hours, sometimes all day.

One of our heroes was a young man named Flip Kleffner. His father, Sib Kleffner, owned one of the city's two sporting goods stores, and Flip was a good enough baseball player that he was said to have played for a short time in the major leagues. One day after his baseball career had ended and he had nothing better to do, he joined us at Lowell Field and hit fly balls for us to catch. We had never seen fly balls go so high. We'd have sworn that they pierced the clouds before returning to earth at devastating speed. I was camped under one of them and would have caught it except that it fell so fast and hard that it broke through the webbing on my glove and hit me in the nose.

Excruciating pain. Stars and planets! Worse than the pain, however, worse than the blood on my face, glove, and shirt, was that I cried. Crying in shame for having missed a fly ball hit by a onetime major leaguer, I was beyond embarrassed. Flip, however, couldn't have been nicer. He said it could happen to anyone.

Many years later, we met again. I was a reporter on the city government beat. He was a member of the Boise City Council, and he was still the kind gentleman who consoled me on the ball field that day. When other council members were aloof or occasionally hostile, it was Flip who would take me aside and give me a story. If only more government servants were that compassionate and understanding.

Sometimes, in our baseball-crazy kid days, we'd ride our bikes to Braves Field, a distance of several miles, to search for home-run balls in the grass behind the outfield walls. One summer I worked as a vendor in the stands there, hawking refreshments.

"Peanuts!" I'd call out while trudging up and down the steps. "Get yer' red-hot, salted-in-the-shell peanuts right here!"

"Popcorn! Red-hot, fresh-popped popcorn right here, folks!"

That neither the peanuts nor the popcorn were red hot, or even warm for that matter, was irrelevant. We sold truckloads of them.

Our boss was a man whose last name was Hamilton. Everyone called him "Ham." Ham Hamilton. One night Ham told me he was short on vendors and that instead of lightweight popcorn or peanuts I'd have to lug a heavy metal box filled with ice and soda pop around the stands. It was hard work for a kid of ten or eleven. It was also a very hot night. When the game was over, I sought out the privacy of the weeds behind the outfield wall and parted company with my dinner.

Many years later, I wrote a column about being a baseball-besotted boy. A few weeks later, a letter arrived from a reader who said he was passing through town, read it and thanked me for writing about "what baseball meant to all of us." The reader was "Bullet Bob" Feller, who led the American League in strikeouts seven times and is considered to have been one of the greatest pitchers of his era.

Braves Field was a jewel of a minor-league ballpark. The Pittsburgh Pirates, led by Roberto Clemente, played an exhibition game against the Boise Braves there one summer. Sadly, the city tore Braves Field down in the 1960s to make way for a government office building.

We rode bikes to Braves Field, to the river to fish and swim, to the tadpole ponds, to pretty much everywhere. Bikes were our passports to freedom. Playing cards clothespinned to the frames of the bikes chattered deliciously in the spokes.

Summer seemed to last forever. The end of the school year was the beginning of a barefoot, sun-drenched eternity.

Vying with summer for the best time of year was the Christmas season. Grandma Susie would come to visit, often staying for a week or more, filling the house with good cheer and the aroma of baking pies, cookies, and homemade fruitcake. Her prowess as a chef and baker had gotten her the cooking job at the Old Soldiers Home, and she was happy to put it to use during the holidays.

One morning she was casually chatting with my mother in the kitchen while they were preparing breakfast when pandemonium struck, instantly changing what had been a relaxed morning into bedlam. Grandma Susie was standing in what my mother had christened "the breakfast nook," the part of the kitchen with the China closet and table. It was separated from the rest of the kitchen by a chest-high divider. The divider had a built-in bread board, used for bread only in the sense that it was where the toaster resided. While Mom minded the bacon and eggs sizzling on the stove, Grandma Susie kept watch on the toast.

They stood and talked from their respective positions when all hell broke loose. A shriek, followed by exclamations of "Oh, no!" and "Oh, my goodness!" (No one would have dreamed of swearing.)

A cloud of acrid-smelling smoke.

Instant panic.

Grandma Susie normally wore her long hair up in a bun on top of her head, but on this particular morning she was still in her robe and night gown with her hair down. I was surprised at how long it was, reaching nearly to her waist. Long enough to get caught and catch fire in the toaster, a fact she became aware of only after her smoldering locks had become a highly successful inferno. The ensuing scene resembled a football game, with my mother, sister, and me converging on the poor woman simultaneously, all but tackling her in our efforts to extinguish the blaze with dish towels, napkins, the newspaper, whatever was at hand.

Her reaction surprised us all. Most people would have gone straight to a bathroom mirror to inspect the damage. Grandma Susie couldn't have cared less about how it looked. She picked herself up, sat herself down on a kitchen chair, and laughed until tears rolled down her cheeks.

"I've lived through a lot of things," she said, "but this is the first time I've ever caught my hair on fire! And the way you all came after me! My land, I haven't had anything that funny happen to me in years!"

That was Grandma Susie, laughing once again in the face of life's adversities. She remained the positive, cheerful soul she'd always been, living independently in her little house in the farming community of Notus, Idaho, until her death at ninety-two. All who knew her remember her affectionately.

Some of my favorite memories are of those long ago Christmases spent with her: the living room bathed in the glow of the old-fashioned Christmas-tree lights, George Melanchrino and his orchestra's "Christmas Joy" album playing on the phonograph, the aromas of freshly baked fruitcake filling the house. My father's signature Tom and Jerrys lending a tantalizing aroma, everyone mellow and merry, snow falling in the yellow glow of the old-fashioned streetlight on a perfect Christmas

Eve. I still think of those times now and then when I have trouble falling asleep.

Though it was far from rivaling Christmas or Thanksgiving, Decoration Day was a holiday to be savored. (The name wasn't changed to Memorial Day until 1967.) It was the day of the annual trip to Aunt Amy's and Uncle Adolph's house to decorate the graves of relatives buried in the little cemetery near the rural town of Star, Idaho.

Aunt Amy was my mother's aunt, great-grandmother Susie's daughter. She was my only surviving aunt and one of only a few surviving relatives on my mother's side of the family. Aunt Nellie had died at twenty while being operated on for appendicitis. Susie's other daughter, my Grandmother Faye, died of pneumonia, also before I was born. Grandma Susie's only son, Will, died young for a reason I never knew. My mother's brothers lived in California and were rarely seen, so aside from Grandma Susie, Aunt Amy and her family were about the only relatives on my mother's side of the family that I saw much of during my childhood.

Aunt Amy's husband was Adolph Schneckloth, a German American farmer. They had two sons, Edward and Weldon. Edward married, left the struggling family farm near Star and settled in western Washington, but the rest of the family stayed on the farm all their lives.

Hard-working but poor, they lived a half-hour drive from Boise but came from another world. They visited us once or twice a year, emerging from their ancient Austin looking for all the world like characters from *The Grapes of Wrath*. Adolph and Weldon, both white-haired, wore bib overalls, farm boots, and worn work shirts. Aunt Amy habitually dressed in faded print dresses, old-fashioned shoes, nylons with seams down the back, and an apron. (Think Auntie Em in *The Wizard of Oz*.) Adolph and Weldon got up at dawn every day to milk the cows and spent the rest of their long work days doing chores while Amy cooked, cleaned house, tended the garden, canned fruits and vegetables, and otherwise worked from dawn to dusk.

Many years later, Weldon made news in a heart-breaking way. Adolph and Amy had been dead for some time, and he was living alone on what was left of the family farm. Too poor to buy hay, he tried to get his cows through the winter on straw. Some of them died, and news stories about the farmer who let his cows starve made him even more of a recluse than he already was. I was a columnist at *The Statesman* by then, so I went to see him to get his side of the story. He had walled off the kitchen from the rest of the house to economize on firewood and kept warm by sitting next to the wood-burning Monarch stove, his only source of heat. The house by then was all but falling down around him. He economized on words as well, answering my questions in partial sentences that tore at my heartstrings.

"Couldn't afford hay. Tried to get by with straw. Didn't work."

No one in our family was ever wealthy. Almost everyone was middle class. Uncle Allen toward the end of his life qualified as low income. Uncle Weldon alone was dirt poor. He soon followed his cows in death.

Though the Schneckloths' house was little more than a shack—small, dark, rundown, old-fashioned even by the standards of the day—their yard was expansive and beautiful. It was shaded by large trees and brightened by Aunt Amy's gladioli, irises, and columbines. It was there that the annual Decoration Day picnic was held.

Like her mother, Aunt Amy was a marvelous cook, her culinary skills never more evident than on the day the relatives gathered to pay respects to those who had gone before and enjoy the feast that followed. The main course, Amy's Southern Fried Chicken, began in the barnyard with her barking orders for me to chase down the victims. Apprehended, they were taken to the chopping block, an old tree stump, where she lopped off their heads with a hatchet. Plucking and cleaning completed, they were taken to the kitchen, where she worked her magic with flour and seasonings and placed them in the Majestic's oven. While this may sound barbaric to young people with only a vague idea of where their food comes from, it was the way things were done on farms then. And Aunt Amy's fried chicken remains in memory the best fried chicken I've ever had. The Memorial Day feast in her lovely yard, with her fried chicken, delicious side dishes, and dessert of freshly baked pie and homemade ice cream, was a culinary feat rivaling Thanksgiving dinner. I can hardly think of it without salivating.

Memorial Day may have been the beginning of endless summer, but Labor Day brought its cruel ending and the beginning of yet another school year.

School was Saint Mary's, a two-story red brick building next door to a church of the same name. Public school students attended Lowell Elementary School, a block away. Most of the kids in our part of the neighborhood came from Catholic families and as such were destined for eight years of Catholic education under the auspices of ruler-wielding nuns.

It's an understatement to say that my elementary education did not begin with my making a favorable impression on my teacher. My birthday was two days past the deadline for entering first grade. Strictly speaking, the principal should have waited another year before admitting me. With my birthday so close to the deadline, however, an exception was made and I was allowed to start classes. "Forced" to start classes was my take on it. Angry because my friends who were lucky enough to be a few weeks or months younger were playing while I was cooped up in a hot, stuffy classroom, I took out my frustrations on the obvious target: our teacher, Sister Celistine.

She was an old-school Benedictine, black habit, white wimple, dangling rosary. As she passed my desk, perhaps looking for a slingshot, comic book, or other contraband, I did something that in retrospect seems both rash and, because I normally was shy and reserved at school, wildly uncharacteristic.

I tripped her.

Aerodynamically, it was something to see. She described a perfect arc, sailing down the aisle almost as if in slow motion, her arms spread out like wings, her black gown billowing behind her. A large black bird gliding to a hard landing. The room fell silent, the other students staring in disbelief. I hardly believed it myself.

Nuns of the era were notorious for rapping students' knuckles with rulers. Sister Celistine's spectacular-but-brief flight ended with her picking herself up and, with as much dignity as she could muster, extracting a metal-edged wooden ruler from the depths of her black habit and breaking it over my head. This would have been in roughly the first five minutes of first grade. The nuns of Saint Mary's didn't have any trouble with me for the rest of that year.

Aside from the Carved Desk Fiasco.

Bored in class one day, I used my pocket knife to carve my name on my desktop. It was slow going, taking long enough that I was unable to finish before being caught.

"What's that?" our teacher asked, pointing a bony finger at the "Tim W" on the desktop.

Only then did the seriousness of the situation become apparent. Serious enough that she escorted me to the principal's office, who judged the offense to be above her pay grade and marched me to the rectory next door. The rectory was the home of Father John Creegan, the church's pastor and the nominal head of the school. He had come to Boise from his native Ireland and spent his entire career as the pastor of Saint Mary's. I was told that as a young priest he was strikingly handsome and much admired by the ladies of the parish. He was also the undisputed authority figure in matters of both church and school.

Father Creegan had someone else in his office when the principal delivered me there, so there was no choice but to sit in a chair in a hallway and wait for what felt like most of the morning. When at last the door opened and he asked me to take a seat, I was beyond nervous. It was a hot day. I was on the verge of fainting and inordinately moist.

Father Creegan tried and failed to suppress a smile.

"Let me get this straight," he said. "You carved your name on your desk?"

"Yes, Father. Well, at least part of it."

"Part of the desk?"

"No. Part of my name."

A heavy silence. A stifled chuckle.

"And you thought you *wouldn't get caught?*"

With those words, the utter stupidity of what I had done became obvious.

"I'm sorry, Father."

"Go on. Get out of here."

No punishment! It was clear, to both of us, that the lesson had been learned. As I walked the hallway from his office to the front door, I could hear him laughing.

Not everything at school was laughable. Half of our teachers during our eight years there were, in my opinion, certifiable. We had the same one from third through fifth grade, a nun who had made a paddle out of three-quarter-inch plywood and painted a face with tears on it. She called it her "boo-hoo stick," and used it liberally. One boy stood out as her primary target. Check marks noting demerits were written on the blackboard during the school day. Enough demerits and you had a date with the boo-hoo stick, dropping your pants and bending over for what the sister judged to be the proper number of swats. The unfortunate lad was beaten multiple times a week for three school years. If she did that today, she'd go to prison.

Another nun forced us to spend the whole of a school day making fun of two of our fellow students, whom I'll call Bob and Mary. The reason, we were told, was that Bob's parents had invited Mary over for Sunday dinner the day before. Why this unhinged our sixth-grade teacher we never knew, but she made us spend the day drawing demeaning pictures of them and writing cruel things about them on the chalkboard. We all knew it was wrong, but this was the 1950s, when teachers' orders at Catholic schools were obeyed without question.

The victims' parents wasted no time complaining to the principal and Father Creegan because the next day our teacher came to class in tears and apologized profusely. The last I heard of her, many years later, was that she had left the sisterhood and was enrolled in primal scream therapy.

Decades after the fact, I cannot say for certain whether the sexual abuses by priests against youthful victims happened at our school. If so, we never heard about it. I can say, however, that at least one priest seemed suspect. He smoked heavily and swore like a sailor. We liked him instantly. Popular with all the boys, he took us on outings, earned our trust. Then, overnight, he was gone. Nothing was ever said about it. It was as if he'd never existed.

Many years later, I asked another priest about it. Father Tom Faucher, who as a boy attended our school a class ahead of mine, went on to become pastor of Saint Mary's parish and, to universal shock, was convicted of possessing child pornography and admitted to fantasizing about killing a child. A couple of years before his life disintegrated, he invited me to coffee and gave me an autographed copy of a novel he had written. It was about a woman whose father had abused her as a child. When I asked Faucher about the priest who had used such unpriestly language and seemed to fall off of the planet, he told me he had been sent there from another parish where he had been suspected of abuse. Father Creegan, according to Faucher, told him that if he heard so much as a hint of improper behavior, he'd be gone. And he was. When I asked Faucher if he was still alive, he said he was in prison. In time Faucher, too, would be sentenced to prison for having child pornography. He died in the Idaho State Penitentiary.

Abusive priests have caused many to leave the church, others to question their faith. I remain a Catholic despite the crimes of some of its priests and the despicable failure of church leaders to report them to law enforcement. They, not the faith they betrayed, should be held accountable.

The nuns of Saint Mary's were masters of holding students accountable. Troublemakers rarely got away with anything. Part of that may have had less to do with the nuns' vigilance than the troublemakers' cluelessness.

One would think that after having tripped my teacher, having a wooden ruler broken over my head, and realizing the sheer stupidity of carving my name on my desk, I'd have learned to be at least a little bit cunning. Not so. In seventh grade, a friend and I decided to celebrate the end the school year by throwing ink bottles from the windows of our second-floor classroom to the playground below. It was fun watching the bottles explode and the ink form big, blue circles on the blacktop.

Until, out of nowhere, our teacher materialized on the playground, staring up at our guilty faces framed in a window.

"Quick! Hide in the cloakroom!" (The closet where we hung our coats.)

The cloakroom was the first place troublemakers hid. It also had a four-inch gap between its doors and the floor so our feet were clearly visible when our teacher came looking for us.

It was after dark when we got home that night after painstakingly scrubbing ink off of the blacktop, our fingers rubbed raw, and smelling of bleach. Another punishment was waiting at home, where our parents had been alerted of our misdeed with a curt phone call from the principal.

It was at about this time that girls, whom we had more or less ignored during our previous elementary school years, became subjects of intense interest. One girl specifically. A new girl in our class, her name was Jackie Hayes. Jackie was the class's smartest student. She was quiet, thoughtful, dignified. She wasn't older than the rest of us, but she seemed like it. Part of this was due to her temperament and intellect. Another part was that she was pretty, and the only girl in the class with breasts.

Her family lived in a beautiful home on the rim of one of the Benches overlooking the city. Their back yard had a pool. Bill Molitor and I would ride our bikes there, ostensibly to go swimming but mainly to see Jackie. We were, after all, adolescent boys with all of the requisite hormones. To our dismay, we discovered that the girl of our feverish dreams had an older boyfriend who lived next door. He was nice looking, and compared with us seemed unbearably sophisticated. We loathed him.

Many years later, in my thirties, I had a dream about Jackie. She, Bill, some other kids, and I were swimming in her parents' pool. It was the most vivid dream I'd ever had. I could feel the warmth of the sun, hear the lapping waves, see the pattern in the material of Jackie's swimsuit. It was as if we were really there and it was actually happening. The dream was so intense that I couldn't get it out of my mind, so captivating that a few days later I drove to what had been the Hayses' home and peeked over the fence to see if the pool was still there. It was.

That weekend, I went to see a friend who lived across the street from us. He and his wife both had attended Saint Mary's. She answered the door with a question.

"Did you hear about Jackie?"

"No. What about Jackie?"

"She died this week."

I was able to track down her parents, who by then were living in another state. They said that Jackie, who was so brilliant I assumed she'd become a doctor or other professional, had devoted herself to working with the poor in Seattle. I shouldn't have been surprised. She always was the best of us.

Her father told me she died on the same night at about the same time that I was having the dream about her. A friend's take on it remains my favorite:

"Maybe it was her way of saying goodbye."

Unlike Jackie, who didn't come to our school until seventh grade, many of us who went to Saint Mary's were at the school from first grade through eighth, more time than students at most schools ever spend together. We should have been close. Many years later, however, when I tried to organize a class reunion, exactly one student responded. Apparently no one else cared to revisit the days of bruised knuckles and boo-hoo sticks.

Each year of my elementary school education brought increased responsibilities at home. My father believed in teaching kids to work at an early age. One of my jobs was filling the coal hopper and removing the clinkers from the furnace. This could be a daunting task, as evidenced one winter morning when my father uncharacteristically rose before dawn to empty the clinkers. The furnace must have been acting up—coal furnaces were notoriously temperamental—meaning the problem had to be handled immediately. My bedroom at the time was next to the furnace room. I awoke to the sounds of furnace indigestion and muffled cursing. When the furnace room door opened, there was Dad, silhouetted in an ominous, orange glow, carrying a bucket of flaming clinkers on the end of a shovel. It could have been a scene from *Dante's Inferno*.

In the summertime, starting at about age seven or eight, my jobs included edging the walks and weeding the flower beds. Fear of the slugs and spiders lurking in the flower beds made me put off finishing the job for as long as possible, invariably leading to a lecture on the virtues of stick-to-it-iveness.

By my tenth year, Dad figured I was old enough to start mowing the lawn.

He was the proud owner of a Toro lawnmower, theoretically started by winding a metal crank and pressing a lever. This was supposed to have been an improvement on pulling a starter rope. In reality, you wound the crank so many times your hand got blisters and the damned mower still wouldn't start. Toro's advertising slogan was "Haven't you done without a Toro long enough?" Dad failed to see the humor in my asking, "Haven't we had a Toro long enough?" It was a great day when he replaced it with a mower that reliably started on the first or second pull of a rope.

My one and only experience with delivering newspapers was substituting for a classmate for a couple of weeks. It didn't take long to discover that the worst thing about having a paper route, aside from having to get up early, is the threat posed by aggressive dogs. One, a Weimaraner, greeted me one morning by clamping its teeth around my thigh. It didn't bite, but each time I tried to pull away it tightened its grip. My leg was hurting and panic was imminent when I remembered that there were two extra papers in my bag.

"Fetch!" I shouted, throwing one of them to a distant corner of the fenced yard. The dog fetched; I jumped over the fence. From then on, I made a point of throwing the paper to the porch from outside the gate. It was a happy day when my classmate returned from his vacation. Nothing could have convinced me that I would ever work for *The Statesman* again.

My first full-time job was working for the company that Dad and Uncle Wayne started, Evergreen Sprinkler Co. They were a good team. Dad, the businessman, was in charge of sales, the books, and drafting plans for the sprinkler systems. Uncle Wayne, the handyman, was in charge of ordering and stocking the pipe, fittings, automatic clocks, and other parts, and of supervising the work crews. Wayne McAtee, married to my father's sister Helen, was an Oklahoma native and part Cree Indian. He was a master carpenter and jack of all trades, well-suited to supervising the installation of underground lawn sprinkling systems. I considered his onetime job as the foreman of a mine in Peru to be impossibly exotic. He enjoyed regaling the less-traveled members of the family with tales of mining accidents, riding llamas in the Andes, eating tree-ripened bananas.

Helen and Wayne lived in a barn-like house "way out in the country," surrounded by farmland. Dad would drive us there for family get-togethers on a narrow dirt road lined with dairy farms. It was far enough from the city proper that I'd fall asleep on the on the way home. Now the same road is a four-lane arterial lined by businesses, government offices, and a regional medical center.

I joined the crews Uncle Wayne supervised at thirteen and spent four summers with them. It was hot, hard work, most of it on the end of a shovel. Workdays began at 7:00 a.m. and ended at 4:30 p.m., with a half-hour off for lunch. We worked nine hours a day, six days a week. My pay, unchanging during those four summers, was a dollar an hour.

The men I worked with were anywhere from twenty to forty years older than I was, leathery, hard-bitten types who had done manual labor all their lives. Paul, the foreman of one of the crews, was a grumpy sort who rarely had a kind word and was quick to point out mistakes, mainly mine. Maybe he resented having to work with the boss's son. The other foreman, a red-haired bear of a man named Lou Steinborn, took me under his wing. Sensing that Paul and I weren't a good team, Uncle Wayne assigned me more or less permanently to Lou's crew, and we became friends.

By about my third summer on the job, Lou figured I looked old enough to enjoy a cold beer after work. He drove me to a rundown tavern he frequented, vouched for me being of legal age (though I was still years away), and we'd down cold ones after a day of digging trenches. Occasionally he'd take me to his house to sample his homemade wines—grapefruit wine, dandelion wine, and other sublimely awful vintages. I pretended to like them. It wouldn't do to hurt Lou's feelings.

One of our coworkers was a grizzled, nearly toothless man named Bill. Bill had a penchant for colorful weather observations.

"How hot is it going to be today?" we'd ask him.

"Hottern' hellfire."

Or, on a chilly day early in the season:

"How cold will it be today, Bill?"

"Coldern' a well digger's ass in the Klondike."

Lou, Bill, and other members of the Evergreen crews gave me pointers that made the hot, hard work on the end of a shovel easier:

"Don't use your muscles to dig. Use your weight."

"Pace yourself. It's a long day. Don't work too hard or fast or you won't make it."

"Don't drink so much water. Run cold water from a hose over your wrists to cool off."

"Drink hot coffee on hot days. It cools you down better than cold drinks. It works even better if you put salt in it."

I often think of those men, who did such hard work without complaint, and of what they taught me. Because of them, I was able to save a lot of money installing my own sprinkler system and maintaining it later in life. Colorful characters, fondly remembered.

One summer, having had enough of ditch digging, I landed a job as a busboy at a high-end restaurant, learning two hard lessons on the first day. The first was to wear comfortable shoes for a job that has you on your feet all day. My feet, stylishly turned out in cheap penny loafers, hurt so badly by the end of the shift that I was almost in tears.

The second lesson had to do with the restaurant's pecking order.

"I've never seen such a cheap crowd," one of the waitresses complained after our shift ended.

"Me, neither," another replied. "I didn't get a single tip!"

"You're kidding!" I said. "I did great!"

And proved it by pulling fat wads of bills from my pocket. They might as well have been strips of filet mignon strewn before a pack of hyenas. The waitresses relieved me of most of my loot and informed me that they, not the busboy, collected the tips and gave the lowly busboy ten percent

My time at the restaurant was brief. My feet hurt too much, and to the waitresses I would always be suspect. When a cannery in a nearby town ran a help-wanted ad in the newspaper, I applied and was accepted. They'd have accepted anyone with a pulse. The job was, if anything, harder than digging ditches.

The first few days were okay. They put me on the plum line, which turned out to be a test of whether new workers were suited for the more demanding jobs. Work on the plum line consisted of pushing plums around with a long-handled squeegee to make them drop through slots above a conveyor belt. It was boring, but easy.

The corn line was another story. Promotion to the corn line meant lifting four, 32-ounce cans of corn from a conveyor belt, using a tool that held four cans at a time. Your arms ached within minutes. By the end of the nine-hour day, you were exhausted. I lasted a week or two and applied for a job with the Union Pacific Railroad.

The job paid, as I recall, $2.40 an hour, more than twice what I'd made at Evergreen Sprinkler Co. The reason was that it was easily twice as difficult. I was part of a section crew. Section hands, once known as gandy dancers, installed and repaired tracks. My job was to drive to whatever godforsaken stretch of desert track needed attention and spend the day working there.

My coworkers were older and, if anything, tougher and more hard-bitten than my fellow ditch diggers had been. It was the most physically demanding job I've ever had, working long days in the hot sun prying tracks up, shoveling rocks under them, pounding spikes, and whatever else was needed to keep the trains running. Our lunch break was half an hour, which passed in a blink. One day after bolting my food, I stretched out for what was left of the break and fell asleep. In what seemed like a nanosecond later, I was awakened by a prod in the ribs with a shovel. The shovel belonged to the scowling section boss, who was staring down at me through mirrored sunglasses. I stared back for a few disoriented seconds, got up, and drove to the Union Pacific office in Boise to resign and collect my last paycheck.

The following week, I was back at Evergreen. Compared with gandy dancing, ditch digging was child's play.

That's not to say that it was easy. Manual labor is never easy. It's hard, it's painful, and it's mind-numbing. By the end of a summer of work, I was more than ready to go back to school.

Some boys' mentors are their fathers. For others, they're teachers, coaches, older brothers. One of the oddities of the old neighborhood was that the second father to virtually all of the boys who lived there was the only man in the neighborhood who wasn't a biological father.

My dad was a mentor in some ways. He taught me rules to live by, taught me the value of hard work, taught by the example of a life well-lived. He was one of the kindest, best men I've ever known. If I'm half as good a man as he was, my life will have been a success.

But with the exception of baseball, a love of which he passed on, he'd be the first to admit that he knew little about other things of interest to young boys of the era. He couldn't swim and would have had trouble explaining the difference between a quarterback sneak and a slam dunk. His handyman skills were virtually nonexistent. He occasionally took me fishing, but I cannot recall him ever catching a fish. Mostly I remember him wielding a bamboo fly rod that looked to be about ten feet long, repeatedly snagging his hook on rocks, and tangling his line in brush and tree branches. He took my friends and me on expeditions to shoot jackrabbits, then critically overpopulated, but other than that he had little or no interest in hunting. He did those things out of a sense of duty as a father, not because he enjoyed them. He was a wonderful father, but he was a businessman, not an outdoorsman.

Nor was he good with tools or virtually anything mechanical, a trait I inherited. The annual lighting of the fire in our fireplace during the holidays was an event evoking universal dread. Everyone wanted a fire, but we knew all too well what would happen. Dad would crumple up some newspapers and lay them in the grate, arrange the kindling and a Presto Log just so, and use up an inordinate number of matches trying to get the wood to ignite. When it did, the room filled with choking smoke. Dad, or for that matter any of us, never could remember from one year to the next how to operate the draft.

Howard Snyder was Dad's opposite—hunter, fisherman, handyman extraordinaire. It was Howard who invariably was called to open the draft before we succumbed to smoke inhalation. He worked as a troubleshooter for Idaho Power Company and could fix anything. His garage was a garage only in the sense that it had two large doors and had once housed vehicles. He'd built it himself, as he had his and his wife's home, and he used it as a workshop and storage area. It was literally filled to the rafters with hand tools, power tools, nuts, bolts, washers, welding equipment, lumber, hoists, solvents, pipes, paint, pulleys … In its attic was more of the same. To the casual eye, it was a rat's nest. To Howard, it was a sanctuary. He knew exactly where everything was and could find anything from a welding rod to a wing nut in seconds. If you needed a clock movement, a telegraph key, or a part for a wringer washer, chances are he could come up with it.

He was arc welding in his garage one day when I happened by and, never having seen anyone do arc welding, stopped to watch. He had no idea I was there until he lifted his welder's hood and saw me, his normally placid expression turning to one of alarm.

"Were you watching me?" he asked.

"Yes."

"Oh, Tim! I hope you haven't sunburned your eyes."

They began to hurt that evening. My mother was up most of the night, putting cold washcloths on my eyes. Bad as it was, the pain wasn't the worst of it. After a couple of days, my eyeballs began to peel. It was like having sand in your eyes that you can't get out, no matter what you do. Howard wasn't to blame, but he felt terrible.

His basement workshop was a neater version of his garage. Everything from screws and nuts to solder and copper wire was neatly stored and categorized in drawers above and around a workbench. Another basement room was home to his fly rods, spinning rods, tackle, rifles, and shotguns.

He helped and mentored every kid in the neighborhood. It was Howard who showed us how to attach playing cards to our bicycles to make flapping noises in the spokes. He fixed our flat tires, helped us build Soap Box Derby racers. He taught us to fish and hunt, fixed anything that needed fixing. Repairs of malfunctioning toys or bicycles were declared successful with one of his signature sayings:

"That'll stop that foolishness."

Howard was forever fixing something for neighbors. One was Ed Chamberlain, the slowest driver on the planet. Anyone unlucky enough to be stuck behind him was forced to drive at whatever speed he was driving, usually somewhere between five and ten miles per hour. One of the results, in addition to countless angry motorists, was a sludge buildup in the engine of his Oldsmobile station wagon, causing it to run roughly.

"It's the way you drive that's the problem, Ed," Howard told him. "You need to get out and drive it fast to burn the carbon out."

"Well, I took your advice, Howard," Ed reported a few days later. "I took that car out on the highway and drove the hell out of it!"

"Good for you, Ed. How fast did you get it up to."

"I told you. I drove the hell out of it! Had it up to forty miles an hour!"

Howard smiled and complimented him on making a good start. I never knew him to be rude or sarcastic, and he probably had other things on his mind anyway.

Howard was an Outdoorsman. Upper case. He rarely came home without a cooler full of fish or, during bird season, ducks, pheasants, geese, or grouse. His efforts to hone my skills as a hunter yielded memorable stories if not food for the table (other than that provided by Howard himself). Truth be told, I was both trigger happy and a lousy shot.

We were hunting pheasants in a brushy area one afternoon when I saw something move in some dense undergrowth and, assuming it was our quarry, blasted away.

It was not our quarry. It was Tandy, Howard's hunting dog. I was beyond thankful that my shot, as usual, had missed its mark.

Howard was generous in his efforts to assure success for his youthful charges.

"You walk down here along the road," he said one afternoon while we were hunting grouse in the mountains overlooking Boise. "I'll climb up on the hill and flush the birds down to you."

I wasn't prepared for what came next. The first bird he flushed erupted from the trees and flew directly over my head. Its takeoff was so explosive and startling that that I instinctively closed my eyes and fired straight up. No one could have been more surprised than I was when a plump grouse landed at my feet.

"Nice shot!" Howard shouted from his post in the pines.

It seemed the better part of discretion not to tell him my eyes were tightly shut.

We were duck hunting from his boat on the edge of a lake early one morning when a flock of ducks flew directly overhead. I stood and shot over Howard's head just as he was standing up to fire. The blast knocked him back to his seat and earned me the sternest lecture he ever gave me.

One winter morning, we rose before dawn to hunt ducks on the Snake River. It was so cold that drops of water splashed from the river instantly froze on whatever they touched. We'd waded a few yards into the water to launch the boat when I stopped cold. Literally. Howard could tell from my expression what had happened.

"Tim, are your boots leaking?"

That was the end of our trip. Howard pulled off my boots and socks, built a fire and massaged my feet. He may have saved them.

A few years later, I was duck hunting with two friends on the banks of the Boise River when an incident happened that ended my hunting days forever. We'd hunted most of the day and had nothing to show for it. One of my pals had such poor eyesight that he probably shouldn't have been hunting at all. When a large bird landed in a nearby tree, he shot and to our surprise hit was he was aiming at, a rare occurrence.

We probably knew that a duck wouldn't have landed in a tree, but we were tired, frustrated at our lack of results, and, as ever, trigger happy. Not only was the bird not a duck; it was a golden eagle.

We were mortified. I'll never forget the shame of watching that fierce, beautiful bird lying in the grass, looking at us as if to say we could shoot it but we could never break its spirit—that what we had done was inhumane and criminal (as it later became). We had to shoot it again to end its suffering. I went home, put away my shotgun and never hunted again.

Howard was every kid's friend 364 days a year. The annual exception was Halloween. For reasons that were never clear, he hated Halloween. Generous with his time and money the rest of the year, he became the neighborhood skinflint every October 31. He hated Halloween the way most people hate the April tax deadline or the Monday after a vacation.

One of the many things he knew how to do that none of the other men in the neighborhood knew how to do was reload his own shotgun shells. A few he reloaded with rock salt rather than buckshot, to frighten away rather than mortally wound would-be burglars or other miscreants.

His Halloween grinchiness annoyed the neighborhood trick-or-treaters, so one year I decided to do something to get even by soaping his windows. As always on Halloween night, his house was dark and silent. I assumed that he and his wife had left for the evening, which bolstered my confidence about writing something devastatingly clever on the picture window of his living room and getting away with it. To make absolutely sure no one was home, I rang the doorbell—and received a shock. The Halloween Grinch had wired his doorbell to mildly shock any kid unlucky enough to ring it on Halloween.

Undeterred, I crept to the picture window and was reaching for it with my bar of soap when a familiar voice rang out:

"Don't touch that window!"

Startled half out of my Keds, I turned around and saw, silhouetted in the crook of a tree behind me, a sinister but familiar figure brandishing a shotgun. No kid has ever made a quicker getaway.

I never knew whether Howard recognized me that night. If so, he never mentioned it. We remained friends until his death well into his nineties. His wife had died a decade or so before that. He remarried and outlived his second wife as well.

I was grown and had a family of my own the night he called in the small hours.

"You'd better get over here right away," he said. "It's your mother. She's acting pretty strange."

Strange was an understatement. Normally a pillar of modesty who didn't leave the house without looking her best, Mom was sitting in a lawn chair in her front yard wearing only her nightgown. Scattered on the lawn around her were rosaries, holy cards, a Bible and prayer book, a picture of Jesus. It was well after midnight.

Her behavior in the weeks leading up to that had been increasingly odd, enough so that at the family's urging she had seen a doctor and been prescribed medication for bipolar disorder. Anyone who has had a family member with a mental illness knows a time will come after the medication kicks in that the patient thinks he or she doesn't need it any more. My mother was a classic case. Later found inside her home were weeks' worth of pills she hadn't taken.

No amount of reasoning, pleading, or scolding would budge her. Sitting in her lawn chair in the front yard in the middle of the night, surrounded by religious icons, she saw absolutely nothing irregular in the situation and was unwavering in her belief that the pills the doctor had prescribed were a waste of time. She also revealed that she would soon be leaving for a monastery in Oregon to marry one of the monks there.

In the no-nonsense fashion typical of him, it was Howard who saved the day.

He handed her a pill, then a glass of water.

"Here, Marguerite," he said. "Put the pill in your mouth and drink the water. It's holy water."

She took the pill, washed it down with "holy water" and allowed herself to be put to bed. She spent some time at a treatment center after that, returning home for good once her condition stabilized. Happily, there were no such incidents after that for the rest of her life.

As I entered my teens and my interests shifted from childhood pastimes to more grownup pursuits, Howard remained available and ready to help. When I got my first electric guitar, he agreed to build an amplifier for it. In exchange, I agreed to prep his house for painting.

The amplifier was a guitar amplifier in about the way that a pile of scrap lumber is a grandfather clock. It consisted of castoff parts cobbled together to produce a signal roughly half the volume of an ordinary acoustic guitar. To pay him for it, I had to scrape and wire-brush his two-story shake house. It took all summer.

At the time, at least briefly, it seemed worth it. I was young, had boundless energy, and was terminally smitten by the idea of playing an electric guitar in a band. The homemade amplifier assembled in Howard's garage helped fuel a passion that would shape my high school years, and, to a not insignificant degree, the course of my life.

CHAPTER THREE
Rock and Roll

S ome kids excel at academics in high school, others at sports or the arts. The thing I proved to be marginally good at, the thing I was passionate about and that separated me somewhat from the crowd, was music.

I was a good but not great student, average at best in sports. And though not musically gifted, I worked hard to realize a dream that began the first time I saw a live rock and roll band. The occasion was a Welcome Freshmen Dance at Saint Teresa's Academy.

Having finished eight years of elementary school at Saint Mary's, most of the kids in our neighborhood went on to Saint Teresa's. One of the first high schools in Idaho, it opened in 1890 as a high school and boarding school for girls. Saint Teresa's was a turreted, red-brick building on the edge of downtown. A coeducational high school by the time I got there, it was staffed by Sisters of the Holy Cross and a few lay teachers.

The tuition was $250 a year, a sacrifice for my parents. Before he and Uncle Wayne became partners at Evergreen Sprinkler Co., Dad had been earning about $400 a month as a food broker. I never knew how much he made with the sprinkler company, but our standard of living didn't change much so it probably wasn't a whole lot more. It was important to him and my mother to make sure their son, and Joanie before me, received a good education.

Saint Teresa's didn't have a gym, so our Welcome Freshmen Dance was held in the gymnasium at Saint Joseph's Elementary School, a few blocks away. I went to the dance with my then best friend, Justin Bonner. Neither of us had seen a live rock band before and had no idea how much our lives were about to change.

We were instantly smitten. Not with any of the girls—that would come later—but with the band that played at the dance that night. Two members of the Squires were older boys at Saint Teresa's. One of them and another member of the group went on to play in an excellent Boise band called Dick Cates and the Chessmen. Roy Orbison had nothing on Dick Cates, whose voice was touched by the gods. Accustomed to my parents' and sister's idea of music—show tunes and Lawrence Welk—we were knocked out by what we heard that night. I already had a couple of Elvis albums and a few 45 rpm records at home, but the concept of boys I actually knew playing that kind of music was an epiphany. And the sounds they were making! I had never seen anyone play an electric guitar before. That that much sound could come from a mere guitar seemed almost miraculous (though the nuns swiftly would have disabused me of that notion). It was love at first sight with the electric guitar. Justin was equally taken by the drums.

I immediately began saving my Evergreen ditch-digging money to buy a guitar. At a dollar an hour, it was slow going. Joanie, who by then had a steady job working at a department store, offered to help. (She also had paid the orthodontist for braces on my teeth because the $500 they cost was more than our folks could afford. She was a good sister.)

The guitar that caught my eye was a black Silvertone in the window of Singer's Pawn Shop, a hole in a downtown wall. There were other guitars in the window, but I couldn't see anything but the Silvertone. It cost $50. Joanie paid half. I took it home, polished it, stared lovingly at it. That I couldn't play it was, for the time being, irrelevant. That would come.

Justin bought a pawnshop set of drums, painted them black and began taking lessons, first from the Squires' drummer and then from a professional jazz drummer known equally for his chops and his discipline. Stories were told of him physically striking students who made mistakes.

My first guitar teacher was his exact opposite, a kindly old man named Emmett Zinn. Emmett spent a month teaching me the names of the notes and how to play "Jingle Bells," not exactly the rock and roll I had in mind. It was hard to imagine Elvis whipping an audience of teenage girls into a frenzy playing "Jingle Bells."

Armed with our pawn-shop instruments and almost zero knowledge of how to play them, we joined our first band. If ever a band was misnamed, it was that one. The leader of the so-called Playboys was a guitar player named Ron Shannon. Ron's mother had married Harry Morrison, the cofounder of Morrison-Knudsen Construction Co., one of the primary contractors in the building of Hoover Dam and other major construction projects around the world. His portrait had graced cover of *Time Magazine* with a caption reading, "Harry Morrison, the man who has done more than anyone to change the face of the Earth." He had a craggy, distinguished-looking face and a mane of white hair. If Hollywood had needed someone to play God, Mr. Morrison would have been the man for the job. I had to pass through the Morrisons' living room one night to get to Ron's room, where we practiced, and Mr. Morrison happened to be standing in the darkened room, staring out a window as I passed by. Lost in thought, dressed in slippers, slacks, and an elegant smoking jacket, he was watching cars pass on Harrison Boulevard, one of Boise's two most imposing residential streets. He turned and looked at me as I walked by.

"Good evening, Mr. Morrison," I nervously said.

"Good evening, son," he said. "Here to practice?"

"Yes, sir."

"Play well."

"Yes, sir."

It was my one and only brush with the man who had done more than anyone to change the face of the earth.

A friend who occasionally practiced with us, Dean Jackson, had a brush of a different sort with him. One night Ron dragged out an old acoustic guitar that belonged to Mr. Morrison. It was beautiful—exotic woods, mother-of-pearl inlays. Dean fell in love with it. He asked Ron if Mr. Morrison would sell it, to which Ron replied that Mr. Morrison obviously didn't need the money, had probably forgotten about the guitar, and wasn't likely to miss it if Dean borrowed it.

He borrowed it more or less permanently, eventually taking it with him when he moved to Florida. He was living in an apartment there when two men in suits knocked on his door.

"Are you Dean Jackson?" they asked.

"Yes."

"We believe you have a guitar that belongs to Mr. Harry Morrison."

"Uh … yes. As a matter of fact, I do. Why do you ask?"

"Mr. Morrison wants it back."

So much for his forgetting about it.

The Morrisons had truckloads of money, so Ron had whatever gear he wanted.

His Fender Jazzmaster guitar and Bandmaster amplifier made my Silvertone and jury-rigged Howard Snyder amp look like, to borrow one of my mother's expressions, "two cents waitin' for change." Justin and I met the requirements, however, for becoming Playboys. We had instruments, such as they were, and we were available.

Our first "rehearsal" still makes me laugh. Ron wanted the band to learn an instrumental called "Mr. Moto," by the Belairs. Other than "Jingle Bells," the only thing I'd learned how to play by then was the signature guitar line in Henry Mancini's "Peter Gunn" theme song. While Justin beat the drums and Ron butchered the lead guitar part in Mr. Moto, I happily whanged away at "Peter Gunn."

"Wait, everybody stop!" Ron shouted.

"Why? What's wrong?"

"What are you playing?" he asked me.

"This," I replied, playing "Peter Gunn" with shaky fingers and a growing sense that something was amiss.

"That's 'Peter Gunn,'" Ron said. "We're doing 'Mr. Moto.'"

"Yeah, but doesn't it sound okay if I play what I'm doing along with what you're doing?"

"No, it doesn't."

"Why not?"

"Because 'Mr. Moto' is in D, and 'Peter Gunn' is in E."

Regrettably, Mr. Zinn's lessons hadn't advanced to the point of teaching me anything about songs being played in different keys. I had no idea what a key was, let alone that the simultaneous playing of music in two different keys resulted in something resembling Chinese opera. It was a valuable if embarrassing lesson. I left the rehearsal red-faced and vowing to find a different guitar teacher.

My second teacher was more to my liking. He taught me a John Loudermilk song popularized by Chet Atkins called "Windy and Warm" and some tunes by the Ventures, the band that launched a thousand guitar bands. I wore the grooves off of Ventures albums. Justin continued to take lessons and practice drums, and soon the Playboys were doing a couple of actual gigs.

Not that they amounted to much. The first was at the Idaho Children's Home, an orphanage. All I remember about it was that we wore black pants and blue-and-white striped shirts copied from the cover of a Beach Boys album and played a song called "Walk Right In," by the Rooftop Singers. The other gig was at Kirkham

Hot Springs, about an hour and a half's drive from Boise over a mountain pass. Ron drove us there in his souped-up Chevy, never driving the speed limit if he could avoid it. We were lucky not to have sailed off of an embankment on one of the hairpin turns.

When the Beach Boys' song of the same name hit the charts, Ron's mother bought him a Chevrolet 409. I was with him when he picked it up at the dealership. The salesman must have known about his penchant for fast driving.

"I'm warning you, Ron," he said. "It will damage the engine if you wind it out too much too soon. Don't get it over 2,000 rpms for the first 600 miles."

He had it red-lined in the first couple of blocks.

Justin and I never intended for the Playboys to be more than a way to get some experience before starting our own band, the band that mattered. We named *that* band "The Mystics" for no better reason than we thought it sounded cool. There was absolutely nothing mystical about us.

The original Mystics cut their teeth playing for a couple of small parties and on a local daytime television program. I was tired of the name within a few months, but it stuck—literally—for life. Decades later, all the original members of the group but me have come and gone. More than thirty people have been in the band, many of them professional musicians, and its name is still the Mystics.

There are moments in life you don't forget. One of mine was my first look at my first good guitar.

The Silvertone had been okay for learning the basics, but it was what it was—a cheap, pawnshop guitar. For months I'd fantasized about owning a guitar like one on the cover of a Ventures album. Fender Stratocasters are one of the two most popular electric guitars ever made, the choice of Jimi Hendrix, Eric Clapton, and other guitar heroes. One of the Ventures played a Stratocaster, but the guitar that mesmerized me was their other guitarist's guitar, a Fender Jazzmaster. My obsession with Jazzmasters had nothing to do with tone or playability. I just liked the way they looked. The shape and overall look of a Jazzmaster was, to me, almost as beautiful as the shape of a beautiful woman, and for a teenage boy that's saying something. I used to sit in school drawing Jazzmasters during study hall.

A new Jazzmaster with a hard-shelled case cost $402, a formidable sum for a kid who was making a buck an hour. I saved my money in a little wooden box with "Jazzmaster $" carved on its lid. After saving for over a year, I was still $150 short. My parents, knowing how badly I wanted the instrument (I talked about it incessantly), hinted that they might be willing to help out a little.

On Christmas morning in 1962, several lackluster gifts were waiting for me under the tree. Figuring Dad had had a bad year, I was trying not to look disappointed when Mom pointed to something previously unnoticed amid the wrappings.

"What's that?" she asked.

"What's what?"

"That string under the tree."

A string of red twine meandered from the tree through the wrappings to the hallway that led to my room.

"Why don't you follow it and see where it goes?" Mom said.

Suspecting where it might lead but not daring to get my hopes up too much, I followed the string to where it disappeared under my bed, reached underneath, and there it was. The second my fingers touched the case I knew that my folks had given me the best gift I could possibly have received.

I opened the case—the new hinges opened stiffly—and was first conscious of the fragrance—precisely the right word. "Smell" or "odor" are lesser words, insufficient words. A new guitar has a fragrance as tantalizing as expensive perfume. The inside of the case was lined with red velvet, and on this regal padding lay the dream—an untouched jewel with a gleaming sunburst finish, tortoise-shell pick guard, and a rosewood fingerboard culminating in the signature Fender headstock. It was almost too beautiful to touch. I've received countless gifts since then, some far more expensive, but for momentary perfection none have compared.

Unfortunately, it didn't take long to learn that I should have gone with a Stratocaster. There's a reason so many great guitarists use them. They sound great for rock and roll and blues. Jazzmasters have a mellower tone. I sold mine after playing it for a couple of years and bought a Gretsch guitar like the one played by George Harrison of the Beatles. Today, either would be worth ten times what they cost new. Some electric guitars from that era are worth six figures now. As with many things in life, knowledge of that came too late. If I'd kept all the guitars I've owned through the years, they'd be worth as much as my house. One, a 1954 Stratocaster—one of the first thousand ever made—would be worth as much as or more than my house all by itself. I sold it for $900. Thinking about it almost makes me weep.

Musicians came and went during the Mystics' formative stages. One who would stay with the group for many years was one of its more colorful characters. Having heard that we were looking for a piano player, he accosted me one day at my high school locker to ask if I'd be interested in having him join the band. I could not have been more interested. His name was Vance Shirley.

At our first rehearsal, we knew we had something. The group with Vance, Justin, Dean Jackson, and Scott Eberhart would be the first Mystics band to stay together more than a couple of months, the first to get paid to play, the first to make something of a name for itself.

By then I was a junior at Boise High School. At the beginning of our junior year, Justin and I and a friend of ours left Saint Teresa's. We didn't leave because it was a bad school. It was, in fact, an excellent school. Our math and science teacher, Sister Clare Assisi, was one of the two best teachers I had from first grade all the way through college. She had a way of explaining complicated algebra and geometry problems in such a way that that they floated in effortlessly, even for a right-brained person like me.

I went to my first high school prom at Saint Teresa's with a sweet girl named Teresa Dickerson. It took several hours for me to work up the courage to call and ask her for the date, with Joanie alternately encouraging me and berating me for cowardice.

I played on the Saint Teresa's football team as a 135-pound lineman. We played other small schools in other towns and rarely won a game. One of the older players on our team was dating one of the prettiest girls in the school. At a party one night, someone asked him if he intended to marry her. I'll never forget his response. He said he loved her, but that he was going to marry a better-connected girl and become governor of Idaho—which was precisely what he did.

Saint Teresa's had been good for me. I learned academics there at least as well as the kids at public schools had and learned to respect both teachers and other students. The worse dressing down I ever had until joining the Navy and going to boot camp came from a Saint Teresa's English teacher. She was the equal of any drill sergeant in berating me for tripping a fellow student in class. (The lesson learned from tripping Sister Celestine in first grade apparently had worn off.)

Maybe it would been better to have stayed at Saint Teresa's, but we wanted out. We'd had ten years of parochial schools. Ten years of small, insulated schools where everybody knew everybody. We wanted to be out in the real world. So, after the first day of classes in what would have been our junior year at Saint Teresa's, we marched over to Boise High School and enrolled there.

We did not consult our parents before committing the mutiny, which in retrospect seems uncharacteristically daring. To our surprise and relief, none of them objected, at least not very much. We'd had a decade of parochial school education and were seventeen years old, old enough that they must have decided we were sufficiently grounded and knew what we were doing.

Vance was the final piece of the puzzle that would unleash our band on teenagers throughout southern Idaho. We weren't the best Mystics band ever, but none of the evolutions that followed had as much fun as that one did. We were teenagers on our own on the open road, headed to places we'd never been to play rock and roll for audiences hungry for it. For a group of rock-star wannabes, nothing could have been better.

To get to our gigs, we used our own cars or occasionally those of our parents, who let us borrow them when we were in a pinch. They knew how much the band meant to us and rightly reasoned that it was keeping us out of trouble. Between studying for school, rehearsing, and traveling to our dances, there wasn't a lot of time to get in trouble. My mother's car at the time was an underpowered Ford Falcon station wagon. I still laugh remembering the time we drove it up a long, steep hill near Glenns Ferry, Idaho, pulling a U-Haul trailer with our gear. By the time we reached the summit, we could have walked as fast as the struggling Falcon was moving.

Not good enough yet to play at the popular teenage ballrooms in Boise, we went wherever audiences would have us, often small towns—Glenns Ferry, Eden, Buhl, Hagerman, Jerome …. We hired a disc jockey at one of the popular rock and roll stations to be our manager. Listeners knew him as Deacon Del Chapman, though he was not and had never been a deacon at any church. He just liked the alliteration. For a ten percent commission, Del got us gigs at venues in towns from Pocatello, Idaho, to Prineville, Oregon. The venues could be anything from Independent Order of Odd Fellows (IOOF) Halls to high school gymnasiums.

Booked to play a prom at a high school in a little town about two hours drive from Boise one Saturday night, we arrived to find the school locked, dark, silent. We drove back to Boise rightly indignant and went straight to the radio station where Del was working the night shift to find out what had gone wrong. It turned out that the prom in the town we'd spent four hours driving to and from was actually scheduled for the following Saturday night. Del felt terrible and apologized profusely. Then he did something none of us would forget.

"You guys have been looking for a gimmick to distinguish yourselves from the other bands in Boise, right?" he asked us.

Right. We'd have done anything short of playing naked to distinguish ourselves from the other bands in Boise.

"I got a record today by a band from England," he said. "Their gimmick is to let their hair grow long and flop down on their foreheads. I'll play their record for you."

It was like nothing we'd ever heard, as different as night and day from what we'd been playing up to then.

"What do you guys think?" Del asked.

We didn't know what to think.

"The word is that this band is going to be big," he said,

We mulled that over. I was the first to venture an opinion.

"I don't think they'll be that big, at least not for very long. I think they'll be a flash in the pan."

The record was "I Want to Hold Your Hand," and the group would go on to be the biggest group in the history of groups. I'd be playing Beatles music for the rest of my life.

Justin was more prescient.

"I think these guys are going to change everything," he said.

He either forgot what I said that night or has been too kind to mention it.

Our first regular gig was at the Hungry Eye, a teenage dance hall in Buhl, Idaho. We played there every other Saturday night for one summer. By then we'd purchased some serious transportation, a 1956 Chrysler Crown Imperial limousine. It was seven or eight years old when we bought it for, as I recall, $600. Originally dark blue, we had it painted candy apple red with "The Mystics" in gold-leaf script on the front doors. It was uniquely beautiful and the envy of the other bands in town.

We made a point of leaving early enough for Buhl to have time for a swim at a hot springs along the way. On one of these occasions, Dean had forgotten to bring his swimsuit and swam in his cutoff jeans. They were uncomfortably damp for the rest of the drive so he took them off and rolled them up in the window to dry as we continued down the highway. An incorrigible practical joker in those days, I couldn't resist such a heaven-sent opportunity and cracked the window.

It took a while for Dean to notice.

"Where are my cutoffs?" he asked in rising alarm. Understandable, considering that he was naked and we were nearing our destination.

"I think they're somewhere along the highway about ten miles back," someone replied. (Dean was the only one who hadn't noticed me open the window. The rest of us had all but exploded trying to keep from laughing.)

It was a merry group of musicians who checked into our budget motel that afternoon—except for the one covering himself with the damp T-shirt he'd worn in the pool. It took a while for him to start speaking to me again.

Youthful gags were regular fare. Justin, who was part drummer, part monkey, and part contortionist, was the central figure in many of them. At a restaurant where we stopped for lunch in Ontario, Oregon, he surprised us all by climbing to the top of a pillar with a spinning "Eat" sign. Designed to lure motorists on the freeway, the sign towered some fifty feet above the parking lot. Justin, who had zero fear of heights, climbed the pillar to the sign and balanced on top of it, pretending to be a mechanical figure beckoning motorists. In his sheepskin coat with his long hair blowing in the breeze, he could not have looked less mechanical. Drivers almost ran off of the freeway gaping at the singular apparition.

Justin could squeeze himself into the most unlikely places. One was a cardboard box we found beside the highway outside of Burns, Oregon. The box was roughly a cubic yard. With Justin inside, we carried it into a restaurant, set it on a stool at the lunch counter with two of us on either side and ordered lunch. None of the other customers thought much about it until we started dropping French fries into a small opening where the box's lids came together. When we finished eating, one of the band members dropped a cigarette and a book of matches into the box. When puffs of smoke began to rise from the opening, everyone in the restaurant stopped eating and stared. It was all we could do to keep straight faces as we solemnly carried the box to the cash register, paid our bill, and returned to the limo to giggle and guffaw for miles.

We were playing a Christmas dance at an IOOF Hall in a small town when the power went out and the hall went black during one of our breaks. People lit cigarette lighters and scrambled to find flashlights. Break over, we felt our way back to the stage. Surprisingly, the lights on our amplifiers were still glowing. We strapped on our guitars and were about to start playing in the dark when the stage suddenly was illuminated by multiple strings of Christmas lights—all of them wrapped around Vance. Somehow he had worked out how to turn off the power to all of the outlets except those on the stage, used the darkness to wrap himself in Christmas lights, and turned them on just as we started to play. The crowd loved it.

Our pride and joy, the band limo, was more sedate than sporty. It could reach impressive speeds, however, given sufficient time and distance. It was cruising along nicely at about eighty miles an hour on an Interstate one afternoon when the hood latch gave way. The hood folded back like a wet sheet over the windshield and roof. I happened to be driving at the time, which was unusual as Vance loved to drive and almost had to be pried from behind the wheel. There was just enough space

The original Mystics. From left: Scott Eberhart, Justin Bonner, Tim Woodward, Dean Jackson, and Vance Shirley.

between the bottom edge of the hood and the top of the dashboard for me to see well enough to pull over without crashing. The hood was damaged beyond repair. If you think it's easy to find a replacement hood for a Chrysler Crown Imperial limousine, it's because you haven't tried. The limo was never whole again.

In 1965, we were driving back from a New Year's Eve dance in Burns, Oregon, when a blizzard struck. It was snowing cats and coyotes. To its credit, the limo stolidly rolled on through rapidly deepening snow on a mountain pass—until a tire blew. Vance and another band member volunteered to change it, not an easy task on a slick road with snow deepening by the minute. This was the precise moment when one of the power-window motors malfunctioned somewhat spectacularly, producing a billowing cloud of smoke.

It was also when a call of nature struck. Seeking a modicum of privacy, I plodded down the road and was relieving myself when an unexpected thing happened. It was eerily silent in the snowy woods until I heard the soft, crunching sound of wheels on snow, looked up and saw a dark green Cadillac a few yards away and heading straight for me. We hadn't seen another car on the pass all morning, but there it was. An elderly woman was driving. Her passengers were teenage girls about my age, staring at me with a mixture of incredulity and amusement. Shocked out of my wits by the embarrassing turn of events, I began to run—in the wrong direction. I was running beside their car, heading the same way it was, desperately fumbling to zip up my pants. Any amusement that had previously existed among the Cadillac's passengers vanished. Judging by their expressions, they thought they were being pursued by a deranged pervert. The old woman was lucky not to have driven off of the road in her haste to flee.

I often wonder what happened to the limo. When the group broke up, it became Scott's share of jointly purchased equipment. He eventually sold it to someone whose name he forgot, and that glorious piece of machinery and symbol of youthful adventure became lost in time.

The other band members all had girlfriends and were sexually active. This was embarrassingly obvious on some of our road trips, when local girls were coaxed to our hotel rooms. I wanted a girlfriend desperately but was shy around girls and didn't have a girlfriend until I was seventeen. She was a pretty cheerleader at one of the high schools. We went steady for a year. She was a nice girl, but it became clear as the months passed that she had her sights set on something other than being the wife of a rock musician. She ended up marrying a lawyer who became a multimillionaire and United States senator.

The band broke up in a way that still makes me feel guilty. Because of the snowstorm that caught us in the mountains of Oregon, we were late getting back to Boise for that night's gig at the Trocadero, a teenage ballroom operated by our manager. Given the blizzard and the car trouble, we thought we deserved a medal for getting back at all, but Del was so angry that he fired us from playing there and quit as our manager.

This was at the beginning of 1965. The Beatles and other groups had launched what had become known as the British Invasion some eleven months earlier. It changed the way we dressed, the way we wore our hair, the way we thought. And it radically changed the music we were playing. Up until then, we'd been covering hits by groups like the Marketts, the Wailers, Don and the Good Times, and other American acts. Little was required vocally. Scott and Justin handled the relatively easy lead vocals. Vocal harmonies were all but nonexistent. Then, almost overnight, it was the Beatles, the Rolling Stones, the Hollies, Chad and Jeremy, and other British groups that had better voices and musicianship, challenging vocal harmonies, and more sophisticated melodies and chord progressions. The difference between them and most of the American pop bands that had gone before was enormous.

Justin, Vance, and I wanted to play the new music. The other two members of the group were less enthusiastic about it so the three of us decided to start a new Mystics band. Instead of being up front about it, we lied to the other two and said we were quitting. They knew exactly what we were up to, a fact that became obvious when Dean approached me with one of his Mystics suits and asked whether our new bass player would be interested in having it.

To this day, I regret not being honest about our plans. The five of us had been almost inseparable. We had more laughs, more spontaneous, exuberant fun in that band than in of any I've been in since. I still feel guilty about the way it happened.

Our new bass player was a friend named John Hynes. Tom McMeekan, who went on to be the best lead guitarist I've ever known, was our new rhythm guitar player. The new band gelled quickly, but we needed a venue. The one that came to mind was the Fiesta Ballroom, in downtown Boise. A former Arthur Murray Dance Studio, it was on the second floor of what originally had been a Fraternal Order of Eagles building. It had a good-sized room with a bar for soft drinks, tables, chairs, and couches, and a much larger room with the best dance floor in town. A man named Mel Day had previously leased the ballroom and made it the place to go on Saturday nights when a group called the Chancellors played there. Day tired of the dance business, however, and by the time we were handed our hats at the Trocadero, the Fiesta had been closed for some time. My plan for giving the new band a home was to reopen the Fiesta. I went to Day's home and pleaded with him to do it. He was nice enough, but could not have made it clearer that he had had his fill of running a teenage dance hall.

I was disappointed, but not enough to give up. I was lying awake feeling sorry for myself that night when a bold idea came to mind:

What if we could run the place ourselves?

The owner of the Eagles/Fiesta building was Paul B. Larsen, a local real estate agent. We met at his office. He was open to the idea of leasing the ballroom to us, but only if someone of legal age signed the lease. Legal age was twenty-one. None of us was older than eighteen.

"If you could get one of your fathers to sign the lease, I'd be willing to give it a try," Larsen said.

Dad was surprisingly open to that idea. A small business owner himself, he may have thought that running one of my own would prove to be a valuable lesson. He made it clear that my bandmates and I—and not him—would be the ones on the hook. He would sign the lease, but we were responsible for the actual operation of the dance hall. If it failed and we ended up owing people money, it would be up to us to pay them back.

It was one of the best things Dad ever did for me. Hiring people to take money at the door, run the soft-drink bar, and do the janitorial work was a labor of love, as was buying radio time and writing ads to promote our dances. With our own ballroom, we also had a perfect place to rehearse, which we did a lot. With Justin, Tom, and me doing the vocals, we were able to handle the British bands' harmonies, and by this time we were all pretty fair musicians for those times. The night we opened, the ballroom was packed. We played from nine to midnight and floated home on a cloud of happiness.

It was our time, our turn. We had enviously watched as other groups took their turns as the top band in Boise—Paul Revere and the Raiders, Dick Cates and the Chessmen, the Chancellors, the Hitchhikers and, at long last, the Mystics.

The ballroom wasn't just a place to rehearse and play on Saturday nights. It was our clubhouse. We'd sit on the stage in the dark and tell ghost stories, the old building creaking and groaning around us. We all swore we heard footsteps in the vacant third floor above us. It was deliciously scary.

One Sunday night, I realized that I'd forgotten to take my guitar home after the Saturday night dance. It was an expensive Gretsch Country Gentleman, and there was no way I could sleep knowing it wasn't safe at home. Climbing the two flights of stairs and switching on the lights in the ballroom, I was relieved to see it in its case on the stage. After picking it up and starting to walk back across the dance floor to turn off the lights, though, I felt the hair on the back of my neck rising.

You know that creepy feeling you get when you think someone is watching you? It was that, compounded. Hoping to see one of my bandmates peek out from behind a curtain, I turned around and looked at the stage. No friendly face, no the-joke's-on-you laughter. Just the eerie feeling that someone was watching. As I stared at the stage, my guitar amplifier began to wobble. It was a tall, heavy amplifier. Thinking one of my bandmates was pushing it from behind, I relaxed—until it fell over to reveal the empty space behind it! No one in the history of feet has run faster. I was down the stairs and in my car in seconds, not even bothering to shut off the lights or lock the front door. You'd think that after all this time there would be an explanation. Hearing what had happened, my fellow Mystics were as mystified as I was. It happened on a Sunday night in a deserted downtown. No heavy equipment operating nearby that might have set up a vibration; not even any traffic. To this day, it remains a mystery.

We spent oodles of free time at the old ballroom even when we weren't rehearsing or playing. We bought a baby alligator as a band mascot and kept it in a tub on the third floor. We played cards and drank beer there. We took our girlfriends there, thinking it would impress them to hang out in the most popular teenage dance hall in town when it wasn't open for business. This was not entirely wishful thinking.

My girlfriend during the Fiesta days, due as much or more to the band's popularity as to any of my attributes, was a knockout. One day I fell a little behind her while we were walking on a downtown sidewalk and noticed that every single male, from other teenagers to old men, gave her long, admiring looks. We were together for a little over a year. If not for my being in the band, she probably wouldn't have given me a second look.

The group played Saturday nights at the Fiesta for about a year and a half. On the best nights, more than 600 teenagers danced elbow to elbow. From the stage, we could see the floor shaking. There is no describing the feeling that comes with playing music and playing it well on a night like that—the dance floor packed with happy people, the band tight, all five musicians thinking and playing as one. It was magical.

Admission to our dances was a dollar. With rent, advertising, and what we paid the friends who worked the door, the bar, and did the janitorial work, our expenses were a little over $150 per dance. We were rich. A large dresser drawer in my room

The British Invasion-era Mystics. The picture was taken on the fire escape of the Fiesta Ballroom in downtown Boise, where the group played on Saturday nights. From left: Justin Bonner, John Hynes, Tim Woodward, and Vance Shirley.

at my parents' house was literally stuffed with dollar bills.

Just the opposite was happening at the Trocadero, where Del continued to hire the same groups that had brought him pre-British Invasion success. Crowds there were small. Hoping to reverse the trend, he spent a lot of money to have Paul Revere and the Raiders play at the Trocadero on a Saturday night while we were at the Fiesta. We had what was a relatively small crowd for us that night, about 400, but a friend who went to the Trocadero counted a total audience of thirty-three. Del eventually closed the ballroom and declared bankruptcy.

Many years after that, when a much later evolution of the Mystics opened for Chad and Jeremy at a fundraiser and Del was the emcee, I told him I felt bad about what happened with the Trocadero. I honestly did. It was never our intent to put anyone out of business. All we wanted was a place to play. His gracious response was to say there had been a lot of water under the bridge since then, smile, and shake my hand. I was grateful to him for that and admired him for it. He died a year or so later.

In addition to playing at the Fiesta every Saturday night, we played Friday nights at high school dances or for dances we arranged and promoted ourselves in National Guard armories, IOOF halls, and other venues. One year we played over the Christmas break at the IOOF Hall in Ketchum, Idaho, a mile from Sun Valley. It snowed and snowed and snowed. Three feet of snow. Sun Valley is picturesque at almost any time of year, but that Christmas was special. Snow buried the fence tops, closed most of the roads. No matter where you looked, it was like looking at a postcard.

We'd driven the limo the short distance from Ketchum to Sun Valley after playing one night when we encountered a car stuck in a snowbank. A black Cadillac limousine. A driver wearing a chauffeur's cap and two men in long, black overcoats were trying to push it out and getting nowhere so we stopped to help. You can imagine our surprise when the two men in the black coats proved be Robert and Teddy Kennedy. They thanked us, and we all started to push. I was pushing on a rear fender near one of the back doors. Framed in its window, inches from me, was the lovely face of Jackie Kennedy.

This would have been Christmas 1965. Her husband, the president so revered by young people, had been assassinated two years earlier. Such was our respect for him that when our high school principal announced his death over the school's PA system and encouraged students to go to their respective churches, almost all of them did. It was hard to believe that for that brief moment on a snowy Sun Valley road we were in the company of three of the most famous people on the planet. We were able to get their car out of the snowbank, they thanked us again, and with that they were off to a club called the Boiler Room in the Sun Valley Lodge. We followed them, hoping to extend the moment, but we were minors and not allowed inside.

That was a minor disappointment, though. We'd had an unforgettable experience during an idyllic Christmas break in one of the most beautiful places in Idaho. And the storm closed the roads so we had a perfect excuse for missing a couple of days of school.

The band had its share of local success, but one thing it didn't have that any group wanting to be taken seriously had to have for more than local success was a record. To that end, I wrote a couple of songs. The group learned them, and audiences seemed to like them. Encouraged, we decided to go to California to make the record that would make the world forget the Beatles.

The Chrysler limousine by this time had been replaced by a sea-foam green 1957 Ford Ranch Wagon. This, with a U-Haul trailer containing our gear, would be the vehicle that transported us to our date with destiny.

We left well before dawn. Vance was behind the wheel as usual. The rest of us almost immediately fell asleep.

It seemed as if hours had passed when the Ford rolled to a stop in a small town, waking us.

"Where are we?" someone asked. "Jordan Valley?"

"McDermitt?"

"Winnemucca?"

These were towns in Oregon and Nevada, respectable distances from Boise.

A long pause.

"We're in Homedale," Vance sheepishly replied.

Homedale was less than an hour's drive from home.

"Homedale! What the hell have you been doing?"

Dreamily enjoying life at the helm, he had taken a wrong turn in the dark and gotten lost. Classically exhibiting the male propensity for plunging ahead rather than stopping to ask for directions, he had been driving forever and getting almost nowhere.

Vance was the star in yet another misadventure that day. On a desolate stretch of Nevada desert, the Ford's generator died. Vance diagnosed the problem, extracted the generator, and he and I hitchhiked to the small town of Lovelock to buy a new one.

It took several hours on a day when the temperature was pushing 100. When we returned with the new generator, one of the parched band members poked his red face out of one of the Ford's windows and gave us a wan smile of welcome with cracked lips. He looked as if he'd been parboiled.

Having successfully installed the new generator, Vance took the wheel and we were on our way again.

For about half an hour. That was how long the new generator lasted. The mechanic who sold it to us failed to mention that it was a reverse polarity generator, which probably had been gathering dust in his shop for months. He knew exactly what would happen and was only too happy to take our money a second time for the correct type of generator.

It wasn't as if we had a lot of money to spare on duplicate auto parts. The consensus was that we should drive him back to the blistering alkali flat where most of the band had spent the day flirting with sunstroke and leave him there. Vance, however, had come up with a different sort of retribution.

"Don't worry, guys," he said. "I got us a little something to get even."

With that he directed our attention to a gleaming set of socket wrenches on the floor in front of the driver's seat.

"They're really good ones," he proudly told us. "Professional grade. Probably worth at least as much as one of those generators. Wonder if he's missed them yet."

Vance's nimble fingers were adept at more than fixing cars and playing the piano. It was a relief when we crossed the California state line, beyond the reach of any Nevada law enforcement officer to whom the mechanic had reported the theft.

Our first night in California was at the home of my ultraconservative Uncle Bill and Aunt Mary. On my only other visit to their home, as a preteen, they had told my mother that the Russians would announce on July 4, 1963, from the steps of the nation's capital that they had taken us over and we were officially a Communist country. My mother worried herself sick about it for years.

They also were health food enthusiasts. Aunt Mary greeted us the next morning with pancakes she'd made with bran and half a dozen other ingredients gleaned from her pantry and her extensive reading of health-food books by questionable experts.

"These'll stick to your ribs, boys," she said.

We thanked her and left, feeling as if we'd consumed bowling balls for breakfast. No one was hungry again for a day and a half.

Before leaving for California, we'd purchased beachwear that a salesman in Boise assured us was all the rage on the Golden State's beaches. Clam diggers were basically capris for men, reaching to about mid-calf.

Ted and Will Schubach, friends whose family had moved from Boise to Los Angeles, talked their parents into putting us up there for a few nights.

"What are those things you're wearing?" they asked us on the day we went to the beach.

"What? You've never heard of clamdiggers? They're supposed to be the big thing here."

They looked skeptical.

At Malibu Beach, we were the only ones without California tans.

And the only ones wearing clamdiggers.

We were more than a little self conscious as we strolled single file onto one of the world's most famous beaches, our pasty-white bodies sporting attire that in all likelihood had never been seen there before and hasn't since.

"Shit!" we overheard a deeply tanned muscle builder say to a group of his bronzed friends. "Look at those guys!"

Our stay at the beach lasted about ten minutes, more than enough time to get our fill of stares, glares, and insults. Returning to the Schubach residence, we consigned our clamdiggers to a trash can and set about practicing in their garage.

This went on for several days, long enough for Mr. Schubach to get his fill.

"When I get home from work tonight, I want them gone, Will," he said to his oldest son over breakfast.

He was sitting right next to me at the breakfast table, so close our elbows were touching, but he repeatedly referred to us in the third person as if we weren't there.

"They're bums, Will," he went on. "They'll never be anything but bums. They're eating our food, they're using all our hot water, and they're driving me crazy practicing that stuff they call music in our garage. When I come home tonight, I want them gone, Will. I never want to see them again."

We were, and he didn't.

As it happened, we were ready to leave anyway, having connected with a man in Northern California who was interested in hearing what we had to record. His name was George Martin, an encouraging sign as it was also the name of the famous English record producer known as the Fifth Beatle. Our George Martin was affiliated with a recording studio in Lodi, California. We arranged to meet him and a producer named Arvey Andrews there and drove north for our rendezvous with stardom.

Martin and Andrews liked my songs well enough to record them and finance the several days we spent in the studio. They were pleased with the results, said they'd start work on pressing the records and let us know if and when they needed us.

Months passed without a word. Worse, the group's days were numbered. Our bass player showed up on my front porch one afternoon and sheepishly confided that his girlfriend was pregnant. They'd be getting married soon and he'd have to quit the band and find a day job. Vance married his girlfriend and left the group a few months later. By the time the much-anticipated call came, the group had broken up.

Martin was calling to say he'd gotten our record played on a "Hit or Miss" show on the main rock station in Los Angeles. Listeners called to vote on whether a song was a hit or a miss. Ours, Martin said, was five-to-one hit.

"I want you guys to come back to California and go on tour with another group I'm promoting called the Golliwogs," he said.

Golliwogs? What kind of a name was that?

"I'll be with you on the tour to judge audience reaction," he went on. "Whichever group audiences react most favorably to is the one I'll promote."

The break we'd dreamed of for years. Ruefully, I told Martin the group no longer existed.

Then I hung up the phone and cried.

The Golliwogs must not have thought much of their name, either. They changed it to Creedence Clearwater Revival and went on to sell 28 million records.

Regrets about the path not taken? A few. That said, dwelling on missed opportunities never accomplishes anything, and who knows? The path not taken might have been a nightmare. Rock and roll history is rife with stories of artists destroyed by success. For every Paul McCartney or Jimmy Buffett there are scores of Jim Morrisseys and Kurt Cobains. And things worked out okay. People still remember the Mystics at the Fiesta, and those were some of happiest times of our lives.

Nothing lasts forever, of course. Even Justin, the band's cofounder, had left the group the previous year to join an excellent band called the Quirks. We replaced him and continued to draw respectable crowds on Saturday nights while the Quirks packed a dance hall next door on Friday nights.

One of the Quirks drove an old Nash Ambassador that was absolutely silent. It could pass within a few feet of you and if you weren't looking in the right direction you'd never know it was there. One afternoon while reading a book in my parents' living room, I was surprised to see it glide up to the curb in front of the house. Out piled all but one of the Quirks. Clearly, something unusual was up. We were, after all, rival bands. Social calls weren't part of the protocol.

I could not have been more surprised when they said they wanted to replace their bass player and wondered whether I'd be interested. Flattering as the offer was, I declined. I was a guitar player, not a bass player, and my band was the Mystics. By then I was its only original member, and it remained the most important thing in my life. There was no way I'd leave it.

The end was in sight, though. The drummer who replaced Justin was getting serious about the girl he eventually would marry and wanted to spend more time with her and less time rehearsing. With the Vietnam war and the draft heating up, I joined the Navy Reserve.

A few months later, a local dance hall operator named Larry Tiegs tracked me down in the library at Boise Junior College, where I was a struggling sophomore, and said that Paul Revere was interested in having me audition for his band. By then Paul Revere and the Raiders had rebounded from the British Invasion malaise that afflicted so many American groups and were on their way to becoming a national act. It was the opportunity of a lifetime, but with two years of active duty approaching I had no choice but to decline. I might not have passed the audition anyway, and in any case I was spared having to go onstage wearing a Revolutionary War costume.

The early Mystics, for the most part, proved Mr. Schubach wrong. Not even Vance would have qualified as a bum. He went through numerous low-level jobs and failed relationships, ultimately drinking himself to death while relatively young. But he always worked, kept a roof over his head, and paid his bills. He was funny, good-hearted, and smart enough that with more ambition he could have been anything from a crackerjack mechanic to an engineer. I still miss him.

Dean Jackson went on to become a fighter pilot in the Idaho Air National Guard and later a corporate pilot and air ambulance pilot. He's been happily married to the same woman for many years.

John Hynes, the bass player who replaced Dean, never got a degree but went from working as a manual laborer in a sawmill to managing multiple sawmills in Washington state, supervising some 400 employees. When he retired, he and his high school-sweetheart wife moved back to the Boise area, where they lived in a gorgeous home on a golf course until his death of a heart attack at sixty-five.

Justin retired as the maintenance supervisor for several hospitals in North Idaho. He continues to write, play, and record music.

In the twilight of my life, I wistfully recall the high-spirited road trips in the limousine with the early Mystics and the heady days at the Fiesta, playing hits by popular groups of the time. But that happy chapter was closing. It was 1966, and my teens were ending. I turned twenty that year. More and more young men were being sent to Vietnam, and my number was up.

CHAPTER FOUR
Sailors and Spies

The summer I turned nineteen, a letter from President Richard Nixon landed in my folks' mailbox. I had registered for the Selective Service upon turning eighteen, the war in Vietnam was escalating and several of my friends had received their draft notices. It was only a matter of time until mine arrived, and the time had come. It wasn't necessary to open the envelope to know what was inside.

"Greetings from the President of the United States," the letter began. As if he were inviting me to a tea instead of a war.

Nixon's letter directed me to report for an army physical examination prior to being inducted.

Recipients of induction letters responded to them in a variety of ways. Most reported for their physicals and, if they passed, joined the army and most likely went to Vietnam.

Some failed the physicals. One of my friend's vision was so bad that when asked to identify which letter an arrow on a chart was pointing to, he honestly asked, "what arrow?" Another friend psyched himself into having high blood pressure for the exam. The most extreme avoidance techniques employed were those of a friend who had someone hit him in the leg with a sledgehammer, the resulting injuries disqualifying him for military service, and an acquaintance who temporarily damaged his eyes by staring at an arc welder. The doctors had seen that one before and were happy to welcome him to the army.

The exam could be skipped if one voluntarily joined a branch of the military beforehand. Dad's advice in that regard was surprising, given that he had been a Marine.

"Do you want to be in the army?" he asked.

He might as well have asked if I wanted to join the Rockettes. The prospect of crawling around in a jungle with bullets whizzing over my head was not appealing.

"You should join another branch of the service then," he said. "I don't care which one it is as long as it's not the Marine Corps."

Marines are noted for being fiercely loyal—Semper Fi, once a Marine, always a Marine—but there was no love lost between Dad and the Marine Corps. He never said why, but my guess is that, being so much older than the young Marines he served with—he was forty when he joined following the attack on Pearl Harbor—he had been subjected to his share of grandpa jokes. He was only too happy to spend most of his hitch as an aide to a captain at the naval shipyard in Bremerton, Washington.

"You might want to consider the Navy," he said. "I had a good impression of the Navy when I was a Marine and thought a lot of the Navy people I worked with at Bremerton."

Navy recruiting posters at our post office had made a favorable impression on me as well. I'd occasionally paused there to admire a painting of a tall, handsome sailor in his dress blue uniform, standing on a dock looking at an aircraft carrier while holding the hand of his young son.

Perhaps I could become a dashing Navy pilot. I had almost two years of college under my belt and a private pilot's license. Bewitched by airplanes (I'd spent hours watching them take off and land at Boise's airport), I used some of my Mystics income to pay for flying lessons.

My instructor was a patient, long-suffering man named Jack Huffman. Jack had been teaching for years and had witnessed every mistake a student pilot could make. I made my share, but studied the ground-school instruction book diligently, did my best to master the skills Jack taught me and ultimately passed the exam for my license.

To celebrate, I took Mom and Dad for rides in a two-seater Cessna. They were terrified but went anyway, stoically enduring with clenched jaws and pale faces what was meant to be a joy ride. Knowing how important it was for me to show them my newly acquired skills, they swallowed their fears and graciously refrained from kissing the ground when we landed safely.

Proud as I was my newly minted license, however, it was clear and had been for some time that I wasn't cut out to be the dashing Pan American World Airways captain I'd dreamed of becoming. Born pilots are comfortable in the air. I never was.

Practicing stalls, a maneuver in which a plane is made to climb so steeply it can't fly any more, forcing the pilot to dive to gain enough speed to recover, frightened me even with my instructor in the next seat. Practicing them alone was unnerving and then some. Death was one mistake, one panicked slip-up away. I'm convinced that practicing stalls over the deserts of Southwest Idaho may have contributed to a lifelong fear of heights.

The Navy didn't have much of a presence in landlocked Boise, but it did have a reserve training center. A recruiter there was delighted to see me. We discussed options—regular Navy or Navy Reserve, officer or enlisted—and, lacking enough college credits to become an officer, I enlisted in the Reserve.

Joining the Navy wasn't a difficult decision to make. Nixon's letter was the catalyst, but I was restless to do *something* and had been unhappy as a student at Boise Junior College for two years. I started there as a liberal arts major. Then, at Dad's urging, I switched to business and hated it. A hitch in the Navy would give me time to sort things out. I had no idea what to do with my life and without a goal had little motivation to study for classes that may or may not have been of any long-term use.

My grades for most of the two years were average at best. The hardest course, taken to satisfy a science requirement because it looked like the easiest science option available, was called Physical Science. It proved to be mostly physics. It was so difficult and I fell so far behind that, with a month left in the semester, I stopped going to class. Hoping for a miracle, I showed up anyway to take the final exam. Knowing I'd failed it miserably, I wrote a note at the bottom of the last page:

"Sorry to have done so poorly on this and to have missed so many classes. It doesn't matter much, though, because I'll probably be in Vietnam soon."

It wasn't my intent for this to affect my grade, but the kindly old professor must have taken pity on a lad who was likely to be going off to war and gave me a D. I deeply deserved an F.

Serving in the Reserve would involve a year of attending weekly meetings in Boise, during which I would report for recruit training in San Diego and a two-week training cruise in Seattle. Two years of full-time active duty would follow. The time would pass quickly. Then I could get back to spending time with my girlfriend and playing in my band again, assuming I survived Vietnam. I was only half joking in telling friends that with my luck I'd get shot seconds after setting foot on Vietnamese soil.

Mom and Dad thought the Navy Reserve sounded good, too. So, on the seventh day of August 1966, I signed the papers to become a seaman recruit. The recruiter gave me four aptitude tests. Three were pretty much general knowledge tests. An avid reader with two years of junior college behind me, I got perfect scores on all of them. The fourth, a mechanical aptitude test, was another story.

"I've never seen results like this," the recruiter said. "How can you get hundreds on everything else and fifty-five on mechanical?"

Easy. I'd inherited Dad's mechanical aptitude.

"Maybe you should be in Security Group," the recruiter suggested.

"What's that?"

"I can't tell you because it's classified. But I can tell you that it's good duty. Most of it's shore-based."

I signed more papers and took a physical exam. A few days later, the Reserve Center's corpsman (Navy-speak for medic) called to say there was a problem with my test results.

"The specific gravity of your urine is zero," he said.

"What does that mean?"

"It could mean that you can't be in the Navy. You need to see a urologist."

One of Boise's urologists at the time was something of a legend in medical circles. It was said that the Mayo Clinic occasionally sent him cases. He was also my father's doctor and had performed two prostate surgeries on him, another of my father's conditions I would one day inherit. Dad called and made an appointment for me.

"What seems to be the problem?" the eminent physician asked.

"The specific gravity of my urine is zero."

"How do you know that?"

"From a Navy physical. They said it might keep me out of the Navy."

His demeanor turned icy.

"So you're one of those draft dodgers," he snapped. "I have no use for you hippies. If you came here to get out of military service, you came to the wrong place."

Clearly we'd gotten off on the wrong foot.

"You don't understand, doctor. I'm not trying to get out of the Navy. I'm trying to get into the Navy."

"You are?"

"Yes. I thought I was in until the corpsman called about my specific gravity test and said I needed to see a urologist."

His attitude changed instantly.

"Why didn't you say so? We'll do a urine test."

The results of *that* test were fine. I later learned that the doctor was on the draft board, which might have had something to do with his attitude.

Meetings at the Reserve Center were three hours one evening a week. We learned the basics of military life and studied for our seaman apprentice exams.

Basic training in San Diego was about what anyone who has seen boot-camp movies would expect—up before dawn, lots of marching, drill instructors in your face shouting insults.

The first four days were the worst. If there's anyplace you want to blend in, it's boot camp. United Airlines, however, had sent my seabag containing all of my uniforms to Chicago instead of San Diego. The result was that for four days I was the only one out of thousands of recruits marching around in beige slacks and a black trench coat. I learned too late that I was supposed to have been in uniform en route to San Diego, a fact the drill instructors delighted in reminding me at approximately eighty decibels multiple times a day.

When it came to knot tying, I was a complete and utter failure. Sailors are required to learn an impressive number of knots used aboard ships. I could march, run five miles, shoot, pass the swimming test, find my way through blinding smoke in a simulated ship fire, but knots flummoxed me. I am knot-resistant. I can tie a granny knot, a bow, and that's about it. My brain isn't wired for knots.

"I can't believe you can't tie this knot!" my drill instructor screamed. "A bowline is not a difficult knot to tie, sailor. Any idiot can learn to do it. You must be the stupidest recruit in the history of the United States Navy."

Repeated attempts had the same result.

"That does it," he said. "I'm sending you to the chief. If anyone can teach you how to do this, it's the chief."

The chief, unlike the drill sergeant, was patient, even kindly. We sat on the steps of one of the barracks buildings while he instructed me in the time-tested procedure for learning to tie a bowline: The rabbit goes through the hole, around the bend, back through the hole, etc.

Many minutes passed in this fashion. When it became clear that we were getting nowhere, the chief gently took the rope from my hands, set it down on one of the steps and stared at me with a mixture of incredulity and good-humored exasperation.

"Son," he said. "I've been in the Navy seventeen years, and you're the first recruit I couldn't teach to tie a bowline."

I still can't tie a bowline.

Boot camp provided an introduction to just how exciting Navy life off of the base could be. Four of us took advantage of a day's leave to spend an afternoon in Tijuana, Mexico, just over the border from San Diego. One of the four was from Texas. It's fair to say that Tex had had a bit too much to drink by the time we gravitated to a bar where we were the only customers. All of the chairs were still upside down on the tabletops late in the afternoon. We hadn't been there long when the bartender informed us in hushed tones that the rooms in the loft overlooking the bar were the working quarters of prostitutes. Tex opted to avail himself of their services and went upstairs. Moments later, he burst from a room on a dead run, took the stairs back down to the bar three at a time and plowed through the tables and chairs like a locomotive highballing through a furniture store. Giving chase was a man brandishing a knife. The rest of us joined our friend and ran several blocks before losing Tex's would-be assailant. After catching his breath, he explained that some haggling over price had led to a knife-wielding pimp bursting into the room with threats in Spanish that needed no translation. It was a slice of Navy life that held no further interest for me.

Happily, our misadventures in Tijuana and my inability to tie a bowline didn't stop me from graduating from boot camp on schedule. It might have if the Navy had planned to turn me into a blue-water sailor, but tying a bowline wasn't a priority for those destined for Security Group. Boot camp completed, I was off to Seattle for my "training cruise" aboard the USS *Whitehurst*, a destroyer escort. The *Whitehurst* didn't sail an inch during my time there. There were no bowlines to tie, but the bosun's mate made sure that recruits were proficient in the art of deck-scraping. We did little else.

My first and only visit to the Seattle Space Needle happened during our weekend of liberty. Watching the ground fall away as the elevator rose brought a sense of dread. I began to sweat; my heart pounded. When the elevator reached the top and other passengers headed for the windows to enjoy the view, I inched with my back against a wall to another elevator and rode it down, eyes tightly closed. This was my introduction to acrophobia, a condition that has affected me ever since. Riding in an airplane doesn't bother me, but tall buildings, high bridges, and mountain roads with dizzying dropoffs trigger irrational fear bordering on insanity. Forced to cross a high bridge as a passenger in a car, I'm tempted to jump out and leap off, just to be off of the bridge faster.

That summer was spent working for Dad and Uncle Wayne on the sprinkler crew and counting the days before leaving for active duty in August. For fun, Vance and I tried to start a Mamas and Papas–type group. The Mamas and Papas had had huge hits with "California Dreamin'" and "Monday, Monday," and we liked their sound. We enlisted a young woman named Martha Ames, who could sing, and my then girlfriend, who couldn't. In doing so, I broke one of the cardinal rules of being in a musical group. Never ask your spouse or significant other to join the band unless he or she has the requisite talent. The group never amounted to anything.

With a couple of months left before leaving for the Navy and no musical commitments, I considered buying a motorcycle and riding across the country. The romance of it was appealing. I had enough money left from the halcyon days of playing music to buy a decent motorcycle and pay for my expenses during the trip, but for reasons now forgotten decided against it. I regret that to this day. We almost always regret what we wish we'd done but didn't more than what we did but wish we hadn't.

With the August departure date growing near, it became important to me to try to extract a promise from my girlfriend that she'd be waiting for me when my two years were up. As much as anything, it was an attempt to hang on to the life I'd always known. I'd spent my entire life in Idaho, had never been east of Wyoming and was about to leave for far-off Florida—a place I'd never been and had no desire to go to, to begin a life not of my choosing. And it was entirely possible that Pensacola would lead to Vietnam and all that that entailed. I was scared. I wanted something to hang on to, some solace, but none was offered. Quite the opposite, in fact.

In one way, I couldn't blame her. The winter before, she'd wanted to get married. It would have been a terrible mistake. We didn't love each other, she was mainly in love with the idea of getting married, and we were too young and unprepared. I was nowhere close to finishing college, had no marketable skills and no idea of what I wanted to do with my life. I went along with shopping for engagement rings, but backpedaled when it came to actually buying one. The relationship was never the same after that. Her resentment at my reluctance to get engaged was all too apparent on the day she made it clear not only that she wouldn't be waiting but that the relationship was over. She said some of the cruelest things anyone has ever said to me. It was a cautionary tale on the power of words.

I was upset enough about losing my girlfriend and having to leave home that my mother gave me sleeping pills. Difficult an experience as it was, however, it was mercifully brief. As is often the case, the dread of the unknown was worse than the reality. Getting on a plane to begin a new chapter was the best thing that could have happened.

The Navy sent me and another reservist to Charleston, South Carolina, where we would spend three weeks "in transit," before I would continue on to Pensacola. "In transit" was the Navy's way of getting people temporarily assigned to a base to do the work that people permanently assigned there didn't want to do.

A layover in Charlotte, North Carolina, en route to Charleston provided a steamy introduction to the sultry South. It was so hot and muggy that I asked an elderly gentleman what was wrong with the air.

"What do you mean?" he asked.

"The air! What's wrong with the air? Is there a factory or something around here that's putting steam in the air?"

He gave me a long, appraising look.

"You're not from around here, are you, son?" he asked.

"No, I'm not."

"Well, get used to it. This is the way the air is here."

My travel companion from Boise to Charleston was a fellow sailor named Richard, who had joined the reserve at the same time I did. Charleston was a stopover en route to our real duty stations. Richard, who wasn't going to be a communications technician, would in all likelihood be going to Vietnam. He was one of those people who pass briefly in and out of our lives but leave lasting impressions. There were many such characters in the Navy, sailors who were interesting and colorful enough to be remembered for life, but over time seem almost to have fallen off of the planet. Of those I served with and befriended, I've been able to track down only two. They in turn have come up empty in trying to locate others. Internet searches for Richard came to nothing. I even looked for his name on the Vietnam Memorial Wall in Washington, D.C. It wasn't there, so at least he must have survived the war. What became of him, as is the case with most of the sailors I knew, remains a mystery.

Richard and I arrived in Charleston to weather even hotter and muggier than Charlotte's had been. The heat and humidity there, according to an encyclopedia in the base library, comprise the closest thing the United States has to a jungle climate. It didn't help that it was August, one of the hottest months. Clothes were never quite dry. Sheets and towels never dried. People never dried. The only time you were remotely comfortable was in a cold shower. Then you toweled off with a damp towel, put on damp clothes, and tried to make the best of a damp day.

Charleston is a lovely and historic city, one of the most beautiful in the South. For a couple of sailors from Boise, it was like entering another world—antebellum mansions, cobblestone streets, horse-drawn carriages, history at every turn. With our precious few days of liberty, we visited its French Quarter and Fort Sumter, where the first shots of the Civil War were fired. Mostly, though, what we saw of Charleston was its sprawling Navy base. Sailors in transit were housed in barracks lacking private rooms or anything resembling privacy. Home was a bunk and a locker in a large, dormitory-style room shared with dozens of other sailors, all just passing through. We weren't there long enough to learn much about the base, which was so big it would take weeks just to get to know your way around, and those of us in transit were assigned to the infamous X (menial labor) Division. Our days were spent picking up trash, sweeping, mopping, and doing other mind-numbing chores.

I've been back to Charleston since then and have come to appreciate it for the alluring city it is, but my Navy memories of it are limited to wilting humidity, monotonous work, and listening to Bobbie Gentry's "Ode to Billy Joe," which played incessantly on the radio. Its haunting, rural Mississippi narrative made it a hit and seemed almost universally to appeal to Southerners' sense of place. A lovely song, but it was as if by general assent few other songs were considered worth playing on the radio.

Charming as it was with its cobblestone streets and antebellum homes, Charleston also introduced me to blatant racism. One of the recruits in our transit barracks, who was actually from Charleston, took us to his parents' home one evening for a home-cooked meal. Somehow the dinner conversation turned to the subject of capital punishment.

"I think it's what a lot of murderers deserve," his father said. "Myself, I never killed a man."

Then, with a wink and a chuckle, "At least not no white man."

Another night, we were having dinner at a Charleston couple's home when a woman across the table from me said something that shocked me down to my socks. Up to that point, I'd listened to the conversation without saying anything. When presently I made a comment, revealing myself to be one of the few guests without a Southern accent, her eyes widened.

"You're a damned Yankee, aren't you?" she said, practically hissing.

"What?"

"You're a damned Yankee!"

"I wouldn't exactly say that. I'm from out West. Idaho."

"That's what I thought. You're a damned Yankee. My great-granddaddy was a colonel in the Confederate Army, and I ain't eatin' at the same table with no damned Yankee."

With that she tossed her napkin on the table and left. A stunned silence followed, during which the embarrassed hosts tried to apologize for their guest's behavior. It affected me with equal parts shock and revelation. To me the Civil War was history. To her, it happened yesterday.

One afternoon near the end of my time in Charleston, a chief petty officer took me aside and, in a manner similar to that of an academic advisor offering a scholarship to an elite university, said that my test scores qualified me for the submarine service.

"It's a great opportunity," he said. "It's good duty, and you'd be serving in a vital role defending our country."

Then, the closer:

"Submarine duty also has the best food in the Navy."

The offer wasn't without a certain attraction.

"What would I have to do?"

"With your test scores, there'd be nothing to it. All you have to do is extend for four more years."

Four more years? That was enough time to get a college degree, get married and have a child. Why would I want to spend that much time hundreds of feet underwater in a submarine?

"Let me think it over," I told the chief.

Not that I needed to think it over. The Navy was okay, but being a career military man wasn't something I envisioned, and four additional years sounded suspiciously like a commitment to a career. I thought it over, for about five minutes, and politely declined. The food on submarines couldn't have been that good.

At the end of my three weeks in Charleston, orders arrived to report for my real job. Home for the next six months would be Pensacola's Naval Communications Training Center. It was there that the Navy turned seamen and junior Marine Corps enlisted men into CTs, communications technicians. Because it was classified, we had only a vague idea what sort of work communications technicians did. The Navy nickname for them was "spooks," which sounded a bit ominous, but we were assured that the work was interesting and that we wouldn't regret joining Security Group.

The base at Pensacola was smaller and prettier than the one in Charleston—red brick buildings with white pillars, neat lawns, brooding pine trees. Compared with Charleston, our barracks offered a degree of privacy. Larger lockers, three bunks to a room, space for a few pictures and other things to remind us of home. The base had a commissary, a church, a library, a noncommissioned officers club with excellent bands from New Orleans on the weekends, and a mess hall with wonderful food. Dad had told me the Navy had the best food of any of the military branches, and the chefs at Pensacola seemed bent on confirming it. I don't recall having a bad meal there. The desserts alone were worth the long walk from the barracks. I've since had Boston Cream Pie at Parker House in Boston, where it was invented, and while the Boston variety was prettier it wasn't any better and maybe not as good as that served in the chow hall in Pensacola.

Our training was divided into halves, the first half providing the basic skills needed and the second half the "secret stuff." The reason sailors with other jobs referred to CTs as spooks was because the work involved intelligence gathering, a euphemism for spying, and was highly classified. Students would advance to the second half of their training only after receiving Top Secret security clearances.

Each class had about twenty-five students. The instructor for the first half of our class's training was Staff Sergeant Robert Purnell, a freckle-faced, strawberry blond Marine who informed us after our first day of class that he went on a five-mile run after work and enjoyed having company while doing it, the company being us. This lasted less than a week. Perhaps Sergeant Purnell felt that he had to uphold the Marines' reputation for toughness. That done, he focused on classwork and, occasionally after class, fraternizing with his charges. He took some of us to his favorite watering hole one night and introduced us to what he claimed was a Marine Corps drink—creme de menthe with a beer chaser. If there is documentation of this as a Marine Corps drink, I haven't been able to find it. It's more likely that the sergeant enjoyed a cold beer as much as the next Marine and had a sweet tooth.

The majority of us were selected for the Security Group's "R" Branch. "R" stood for radio. It could just as easily have been called "M" Branch, for Morse code, because that's what we'd be learning and practicing daily for the next six months. We would have to know it well enough to copy it at daunting rates of speed. Daunting, at least, for a bunch of guys who didn't know a "dit" from a "dah" and could have gone their whole lives without regretting it. Compared with riding the high seas on a destroyer or aircraft carrier or patrolling the depths in a nuclear submarine, Morse code was hardly the stuff of high adventure.

But at least no one would be shooting at us.

We were in the first week of our training when Purnell made an announcement.

"It's in your interest to do well in this class," he said. "The two students with the top grades get choice of duty."

Choice of duty?

"Yes. You pick three CT duty stations. Security Group duty is mostly shore-based, and there are duty stations all over the world. The Navy guarantees that you'll be stationed at one of the three you pick."

A goal. Precisely what I needed! I was still feeling homesick, still not entirely over the loss of my girlfriend. Until then, my only goal was to survive the next two years and get back home. But a chance to go somewhere besides Vietnam, where the Navy was sending almost everybody? That was something to work toward.

Everyone wanted to know where the duty stations were, of course. Purnell rattled off some names—Japan, Puerto Rico, Europe, Adak, Alaska, Marietta, Washington …

Washington? I could drive to Boise on a long weekend. The cloud of homesickness began to lift. If I studied hard enough and got one of the top two grades, I could go to Marietta and spend the rest of my hitch within driving distance of home.

It was all I needed to know. I would study harder than I ever had at BJC. I would get the best grades in our class and end my six months in the muggy South by heading home to the Northwest. It was amazing how quickly that changed things. With something to work for, time passed quickly. I was making new friends, discovering a part of the country that couldn't have been more different from Idaho and, to my surprise, enjoying myself. The homesickness vanished as if by magic. With that, the lure of Marietta faded. You don't join the Navy to go home, after all. You join the Navy to see the world, and the world was beckoning. I would study hard, get choice of duty and see some of it.

Between classes, studying and enjoying the company of fellow students, time passed quickly. One of the students was Exhibit A in the case for Missouri's having been nicknamed the "Show Me" state. He utterly refused to believe that my home state was anything but flat potato fields. Only when I returned from Christmas leave bearing postcards with pictures of Sun Valley and the snowy peaks of the Sawtooths did he relent, and then only after trying to rub off the ink to make sure I hadn't had fake postcards made to trick him.

One of my roommates was a young Black man from Chicago. Randall Bland's stories of life in the Windy City made me yearn to see it.

A student name Allen was both the homeliest and friendliest student in our class. Allen's home was on Long Island. He offered to show me New York City if I ever happened to be in the neighborhood, an offer I'd be taking him up on much sooner than expected.

A Marine lance corporal from Louisiana made a similar offer regarding his hometown of New Orleans. We went there on a weekend leave—it was only a few hours away—and the city bewitched me. We drank hurricanes, dined on Louisiana Shrimp Creole under the stars in a historic courtyard restaurant, listened to jazz, rock and roll, and blues played by experts. New Orleans cast a spell on me that has lasted a lifetime.

Near the end of the first half of our training, we were interviewed for our security clearances. Without them, the second half of the training—the classified part—wouldn't happen. We'd be dismissed from Security Group and, for all we knew, sent to deck-scraping school.

We were interviewed for our clearances individually in a private office. The interviewer was wearing a suit, not a military uniform. He had one question for me:

"On the night of (he named a date from the preceding summer), you went to an upstairs apartment at (he named a Boise address) and didn't come out until the next morning. We (no mention of who 'we' were) want to know what happened there."

It was so unexpected that it left me momentarily speechless.

"Could you repeat that?" I eventually got around to asking.

He did.

"You mean someone followed me?"

"Correct."

"Why?"

"We do that with all of the Security Group recruits. If you were ever to be captured by our enemies, they would use whatever they could to get secret information out of you. We need to know if there's anything in your past that they could use. That's why we followed you. So I'll ask you again. What happened in that apartment that night?"

"Well, it was where my girlfriend lived. I spent that night with her."

"Okay. That's all I wanted to know. We (again no clue to who the mysterious 'we' were) needed to make sure you aren't a homosexual. The enemy could use that against you to get information."

It was suddenly clear that the second half of our training would involve more than Morse code. It was intriguing to learn that we could be doing something so secret and important that the enemies of democracy would go to such lengths to discover what it was. Intriguing, and a little intimidating. No one, from the recruiter in Boise to Sergeant Purnell in Pensacola, had said anything about us becoming James Bonds.

We were told that we couldn't say anything about what we did in the Navy until we'd been out of the Navy for five years, by which time it supposedly would be obsolete and of little use to our adversaries. My five years were far from over when North Korea created an international incident by capturing the USS *Pueblo*, a U.S. Navy ship it rightly accused of spying. Most of the Pueblo's crew members were CTs, sailors who had received orders not to a comfortable, shore-based duty station but to the unluckiest ship in the Navy. They were held captive in North Korea until Lloyd Bucher, the ship's commanding officer and a native of Pocatello, Idaho, wrote a tongue-in-cheek admission that they were, in fact, spying. After eleven months in captivity, he and the crew were released. A court of inquiry found Bucher innocent of any wrongdoing.

Time passed quickly at Pensacola. Summer changed to fall and fall to winter with neither fall colors nor snow. It surprised me to discover that even while enjoying the balmy Florida days I missed the change of seasons. By December, with the days still warm and sunny, I found myself longing for the sound and feel of snow crunching beneath my feet. Stepping off of the plane in cold, crisp air for a layover in Denver on the way home for Christmas leave brought happy memories of winter days back home. This was the way air was supposed to be.

My mother was shocked when she and Dad met me at the airport in Boise.

"You're so skinny! Isn't the Navy feeding you?"

The Navy was feeding me quite well, thank you. The twenty-five pounds I'd lost were a result of marching and walking several miles a day rather than any paucity of food.

At home, friends and former bandmates introduced me to a musical revolution I didn't know was happening. When I'd left for active duty, most of the local bands and radio stations were playing music by British Invasion groups, primarily the Beatles and Rolling Stones, and popular songs by American groups like the Byrds, the Doors, and Buffalo Springfield. In the South, it was nothing but soul music and "Ode to Billy Joe." I'd been stunned while watching the Beatles' live, worldwide airing of "All You Need is Love" in the base's noncommissioned officers club to overhear someone say, "the Beatles suck," to universal agreement. In the Boise I'd left, this would have been sacrilege. In the Boise to which I returned for Christmas, everyone was listening to Cream and Jimi Hendrix, blues-based, hard-edged rock music unlike any I'd ever heard, let alone played. If a band was to be part of my life after finishing my hitch, I'd have some serious wood-shedding to do.

Christmas leave ended all too quickly. My folks held back tears the day they drove me, resplendent in my dress blue uniform, to the airport to return to Pensacola. Decades would pass before my wife's and my youngest child left the nest and I'd understand how bereft they felt. With Joanie married, I was the kid who was leaving Mom and Dad with an empty nest. They bore up well under the circumstances, though. They had weathered the Depression and the war so they knew a thing or two about bearing up.

Leaving home when Christmas leave ended brought none of the angst that accompanied leaving home the first time. The unknown had become the familiar. The classes at Pensacola were interesting, I had new friends and not only had gotten over losing my girlfriend but was glad it happened. I was twenty, unencumbered, free to start a new chapter. Rather than something to be dreaded, the Navy had become an adventure.

The first half of our training had consisted mainly of copying Morse code on standard typewriters. For the second half of our training, we were introduced to typewriters with additional characters from the Russian Cyrillic alphabet. Those of us who would be sent to Europe would be eavesdropping on the Russians. We would be learning the code for the new characters in addition to continuously increasing the speed at which we were able to copy. We also learned arcane facts about intelligence gathering, information that seemed clandestine at the time but was reported in detail in news magazines after the Pueblo story broke.

My commitment to studying hard paid off. Graduating at the top of my class, I was given choice of duty and applied for duty stations in London; Edsel, Scotland, and Bremerhaven, West Germany. Orders to one of them supposedly were guaranteed, so it was disappointing at best to receive orders to report to San Juan, Puerto Rico. All eight of the students with the top two grades in the classes graduating at the time— four classes graduated every two weeks—got orders to San Juan. We complained, but the instructors and other old salts who had served in San Juan made us see it differently. They said we'd love it there.

"You won't have to live on a base; you can have your own apartment. You can live like a king on a petty officer's salary in Puerto Rico. An apartment on the beach, a house boy to do all your chores— you'll love San Juan!"

Most of us warmed to

Newly minted Navy seaman. Tim's graduation photo from the U.S. Naval Communications Training Center in Pensacola, Florida.

the idea, but one of the students was unconvinced. He was so incensed by the prospect of going to San Juan instead of Europe that he complained to the officer in charge of procuring orders, a hard-nosed Marine. This struck the rest of us as madness, a surefire way to get orders to Vietnam or Adak, a desolate Aleutian island said to be the worst duty station of all. He had the audacity to ask the officer what kind of incentive it was to guarantee us one of the places we chose but give us orders to someplace else. To universal surprise, he wasn't sent to Adak. The officer agreed with him. New orders arrived soon afterwards. No apartments on the beach for us. We would be going to Germany.

For a twenty-year-old who seven months earlier had never been east of Wyoming, this was glorious news. I'd dreamed of seeing Europe but had no hope of being able to afford to go there until I'd finished college and presumably would have a good-paying job. Now the Navy would be sending me there for free.

The military flight to Germany would leave from Fort Dix, New Jersey. Homely but friendly Allen made good on his offer to let me spend a night at his parents' house on Long Island en route, an offer I was happy to accept as it included a day in New York City. Allen neglected to mention, however, that his parents had not one but five cats, to which I am horribly allergic. I spent the night sneezing, wheezing with asthma, and hanging my head out of a bedroom window for dander-free air on a bitter February night.

The next day wasn't much better. Icy winds swept through the canyons of New York's skyscrapers, making it difficult to think about anything but trying to stay warm.

With rare exceptions, the Navy never seemed to be in a hurry to send anyone anywhere. Before catching my flight from Fort Dix to Germany I spent three weeks in transit (a term that by now I had come to dread) at the Philadelphia Naval Station. My job for the entire three weeks there was cleaning toilets. There were literally hundreds of them, and I must have cleaned every one of them. It was a relief to report to Fort Dix for my flight.

Our first and only stop en route to Germany was in the Azores, but we didn't get so much as a glimpse of those picturesque isles. It was the dead of night in a swirling snowstorm. Our plane refueled there and arrived in Frankfurt the next morning. It was a strange sensation to walk the city's busy streets knowing that for the first time in my life many of the people around me wouldn't understand a word I was saying if I needed to ask them something.

Happily, several other sailors bound for Bremerhaven were along for moral support. That, along with the best beer any of us had ever tasted, helped compensate for the language barrier. We boarded a train to Bremerhaven that night, wishing we'd gone easier on the beer. A hangover is bad enough without being on a swaying train.

The train arrived at our destination early the next morning. Bremerhaven would be home for the next year and a half. Tired, hung over, and shivering in a cold, dreary rain, I wondered whether San Juan might have been a better option.

Our new home was once a Nazi army base. It had been converted to a U.S. Army base, but the Army's presence there was minimal compared with the Navy's. The base was the headquarters of U.S. Naval Security Group Thirteen, charged with naval intelligence gathering in that part of Europe. Sailors far outnumbered soldiers. A few Air Force people were stationed there, but so few that we rarely saw them and had no idea what they did.

The center of the base was a grassy quadrangle lined with tall trees on all four sides. Roughly a block wide and two blocks long, it was reminiscent of an American park. Two-story, red brick buildings, our quarters, overlooked the quadrangle. That part of the base, the part where we lived, looked less like a military base than a college campus. The rest of the base was a mix of other structures: a church, a library, the mess hall (complete with a wall-length mural of a German milkmaid in an alpine setting), a restaurant, a post office, a small grocery store, and a PX (post exchange) with duty-free bargains on cameras, stereos, and other consumer goods. It was possible to spend an entire hitch there without ever leaving the base, which one of our less adventurous coworkers actually did.

My dismal first impression of Bremerhaven could not have been more misleading. Compared with places where I'd spent time in the States, with the possible exception of Sun Valley, the city in those days was impossibly picturesque—spires and steeples; winding, cobblestone streets; quaint shops, restaurants, and biergartens, a bratwurst stand seemingly on every corner. The exchange rate was four marks to a dollar. A beer or a bratwurst with succulent french fries cost one mark. Chateaubriand with sautéed mushrooms in one of the city's best restaurants, a four-masted schooner anchored in the harbor, could be had for the equivalent of a few bucks. We could live quite well in Bremerhaven on our meager pay.

The operations building where we worked was unimposing at best. Maybe that was the idea. Old and dilapidated, it was tucked away at the back of the base. If you didn't have to go to work there, you could spend weeks on the base without ever knowing it existed. It was surrounded by a tall fence with razor wire. We had to show our IDs to gain admittance for our shifts, which consisted of two evening watches, two day watches and two midwatches. Eve watches were 3 p.m. to 11 p.m, day watches 7 a.m. to 3 p.m., and midwatches 11 p.m. to 7 a.m. After standing six watches, we were off for almost four days, from the end of the last midwatch to the beginning of the first eve watch. This gave us time to discover cities that could be reached by train with enough time to enjoy them and return in time for work.

Our usual destinations were the two closest major cities, Amsterdam and Copenhagen. Amsterdam was Dutch chocolate and cheeses, exotic liquors, beautiful canals, and beautiful Dutch girls—few if any of them interested in American servicemen with GI haircuts. Copenhagen was Tivoli Gardens, castles and palaces, a favorite watering hole called the Circle Club, and beautiful Danish girls equally uninterested in us. Our one pleasant encounter with European women happened following a ferry ride across the sound from Copenhagen to Malmo, Sweden. A fellow sailor from Louisiana and I spent a pleasant afternoon with two friendly Swedish girls there, until the sailor from Louisiana put his foot in his mouth. When he happened in passing to mention Abraham Lincoln, one of the Swedes asked whether Lincoln was the sixteenth or the seventeenth president.

"You don't know who Abraham Lincoln was?" the Louisianan asked incredulously. "He was our most famous president!"

"Do you know who Gustav VI is?" she asked.

"Never heard of him. Who is he?"

"He is the current king of Sweden."

So ended any chance we might have had of spending more than a few hours with the only girls willing to be seen with us.

Back in Bremerhaven, it was business as usual, monitoring radio transmissions of the Russian, Polish, and East German Navies. Russian shipping traffic also was monitored, but only by the few techs capable of copying Morse code at the high speeds used on shipping channels.

The military transmissions the rest of us copied were always in code. We had no idea what the messages were saying. That was the job of the C Branchers, cryptographers. They and the translators were the ones who figured out what was actually being said in the messages we copied. We never knew whether any of what we copied was meaningful, let alone important.

On Christmas Eve, we got the collective surprise of our young lives.

"Holy shit!" one of the techs shouted during an otherwise boring midwatch. "Look at this!"

The message on his typewriter consisted of each of our names and ranks—every single one of us! A greeting followed the last name on the list:

"Merry Christmas from the Russian Navy."

So much for secrecy. The Russians knew we were there, knew exactly what we were doing. They were doing the same thing. It was a game. We'd been led to believe that what we were doing was special—top secret, a crucial part of our national defense. The reality was that we were minor players in a Cold War game of Cat and Mouse. It wasn't entirely meaningless—once in a hundred or a thousand watches an operator might intercept a message of importance—but viewed from the perspective of the half century that followed and included the fall of the Soviet Union and democratization of many former Iron Curtain countries, it seems like a waste of resources on both sides of the Iron Curtain. Our mutual paranoia was overrated.

Inspired by Beatle Paul McCartney, who played a German-made Hofner bass, I bought a Hofner guitar from one of the shops in downtown Bremerhaven and briefly played in a band of fellow sailors. Like so many of the people I met in the military, they were from the East and the South and wanted to play soul music. Not having done much of that, I was lost most of the time. It was a question of which would happen first, my quitting the group or the rest of its members tactfully saying it might be best for them to find a guitarist who actually knew how to play the songs. One or the other appeared imminent until one of them asked me if I could play a song by a British Invasion group called the Kinks.

Well, now! I'd probably played that song a hundred times back home with the Mystics and had the guitar lead down pat. They were impressed, and my musical lease on life was renewed. That, however, was about the only non-soul tune they wanted to play. I continued to rehearse half-heartedly with them for a few weeks, then bowed out. They were probably relieved.

The Hofner guitar stayed with me for quite a few years. I brought it home when my active duty ended, and it served me well, if briefly, before coming to a violent ending. More on that later.

Any military base has it share of characters. The aforementioned lad who never left the base was named Ernie. Ernie was from New York City. He spent his entire two years in Bremerhaven without once venturing beyond the base's main gate.

"Ernie!" we'd implore him. "You need to travel! You have the chance of a lifetime to see Europe!"

"What's it got that New York hasn't got?"

"Well, let's see. The Eiffel Tower, the Coliseum, the Vatican, the Louvre, the British Museum, the Alps, the Black Forest, the Mediterranean …"

"None of that stuff is any better than what we have in New York."

There was no convincing him otherwise.

It's fair to say that Ernie was not the shrewdest salesman on the base. When the time came for him to be separated and return to his beloved New York, he sold some of the possessions he'd accumulated during his contented confinement on base. One was a portable record player.

"I'll give you fifteen bucks for it," one of his roommates said.

"Fifteen?" he said dismissively. I don't know … "

"Come on, Ernie! That's as high as I'll go."

"How about ten?"

I have no idea what became of Ernie after he returned to New York, but it's a good bet that he wasn't a hedge-fund manager.

My roommates were Barry and Mike. Barry, from Connecticut, was quiet and pretty much kept to himself. Mike, a Chicagoan, was a Navy version of Jekyll and Hyde.

Throughout our shifts, Mike was the nicest of men—polite, courteous, soft spoken. Smart, witty, a pleasant conversationalist. When our breaks between shifts came, he became a different person. A runaway train. A hard-drinking menace to be avoided if at all possible. Most of us returned early in the morning after working our last midwatch to sleep or prepare for a trip. Mike would be in a taxi headed downtown almost before the sun came up. Once there, he spent virtually the entire break in the bars. His favorite, the favorite of most of the American military people stationed in Bremerhaven, was Zum Schteldechein, or, as it was known around the base, "Sleazy's." Small, dimly lit, and elbow-to-elbow on busy nights, Sleazy's main attractions were beer and a talented German guitarist. Mike would spend his breaks there and in other beery haunts drinking insane amounts of alcohol. He was known to have passed out on sidewalks in front of bars in the wee hours, forcing people to step over him on their way to work.

Barry and I dreaded his returns to our room. He'd burst in screaming obscenities, throwing things, knocking over lockers. It was best to leave during these outbursts for fear of doing something that would enrage him further and risk losing a tooth or having a nose broken. Eventually, his rage exhausted, Mike would pass out or fall asleep. By the time we had to report for the eve watch that began our rotation anew, he was back to being gentle, soft-spoken Jekyll.

A highlight of my time in Bremerhaven was a thirty-day leave that took me to most of the countries in Western Europe. My companion was a fellow CT named Jim Doyle, from Cave City, Kentucky. Our transportation was an eight-year-old Mercedes Benz I'd purchased for $400. It was fine driving around Bremerhaven, but seventy or eighty miles out of town on the first leg of our trip the needle of the oil pressure gauge on the dashboard dropped precipitously. We could actually see it falling. We kept adding oil until we got to an American base in Italy, where Jim diagnosed the problem as a faulty oil seal and replaced it. That bought us another seventy or eighty miles, when the plummeting needle proved the repair to be suspect. We'd stop at service stations and ask the attendants to check the gas and fill up the oil. In Paris, we took the Benz to a shop where a mechanic fixed it properly.

Neither of us will ever forget waking up to the sound of church bells in Paris on a Sunday morning. It seemed surrealistic to be in the fabled city of the Eiffel Tower and Notre Dame, Renoir and Van Gogh, Hemingway and Fitzgerald … It was a lovely summer morning, a beautiful day to be alive and lucky enough to be listening to pealing church bells in one of the most beautiful and historic cities on Earth.

We went to Rome and saw the sights there. Jim, a staunch Baptist who eventually became a pastor, scoffed at what he saw as an extravagant waste of money on the architecture and art in the Vatican. Better, he said, to have spent that money on helping the poor. No argument.

We "oohed" and "awed" at the magnificent buildings of the Grand Square in Brussels, eerily deserted on a misty, moisty morning. We saw the famous Spanish bullfighter El Cordobes in Barcelona, strolled the beaches of the Riviera, gaped at the grandeur of the Alps. Visiting all those places today would costs thousands. We did it with a $400 car, a few hundred bucks in our pockets, and a well worn copy of *Europe on Five Dollars a Day*.

While I was in the Navy, I couldn't wait to get out. Most of the reason for that was what was universally known as military "chicken shit." Are your shoes shiny enough? Is your belt buckle properly polished, your hair short enough? A senior chief petty officer actually measured my hair with a ruler one day before ordering me to get it cut.

Now, I look back on my time on active duty as one of the best of my life. We did work we thought was interesting and important. We made great friends, lived high on low wages. We saw more of the world than many people see in a lifetime.

It ended sooner than expected. In an economy move, the Navy released 30,000 Reservists from active duty early. I was one of them. If I'd extended my active duty time for submarine service or even for two months to get my fifth stripe, I wouldn't have qualified. Instead of the following summer, I was separated in the fall of 1968. I spent a month letting my haircut's "white sidewalls" grow out and traveling: Copenhagen, Oslo, Stockholm, Paris, London. From London, a train took me to Prestwick, Scotland, home to the largest fog-free airport in Britain and the departure point for my flight back to the United States.

A funny thing happened in Prestwick. The train didn't actually stop there. It only slowed down. Seeing me positioned by the door with my seabag, guitar, and an expression of growing concern as the train began to pick up speed again, the conductor told me to jump.

As landings go, it was not graceful. The force of hitting the platform on my back rendered me briefly unconscious. I awoke to a vision of a lovely Scottish girl standing over me with a look of concern.

"Are you all right?" she asked. "Would you like to come home with me?"

Too late, I thought of the perfect response.

"Is this heaven?"

The reality was that her mother ran a bed and breakfast. The beautiful girl who was inviting me home with her helped out by recruiting lodgers at the train station. I spent several nights with them. We watched the BBC on the telly in the evenings and chatted about the differences between Britain and America. They were keen to know about all things American. Like many homes I had visited in Europe, theirs had a picture of President Kennedy prominently displayed on a living room wall.

One night, almost asleep, I was startled by someone quietly entering my room and lifting the covers on my bed. It was dark enough that I couldn't see who it was.

Perhaps my prayers as a lonely sailor had been answered at last.

Alas, it was not the fetching girl who had greeted me at the station. It was her white-haired mother, come to tuck a hot water bottle in under my covers. Disappointing, but sweet. And it left me with a fond, final memory of my time overseas. I was home by Christmas, ready to begin the next chapter of my life.

CHAPTER FIVE
Harvard of the West

I t's an understatement to say that the transition from sailor to university student didn't begin auspiciously.

I came home from active duty in Europe in time for the holidays. Two of my old band buddies were home and dropped by, ostensibly to catch up, but the real reason for their visit was to persuade me to join them at the University of Idaho to start a band.

A lot had changed in their lives during my time overseas. Both were married with children and had made it almost halfway through their college careers. To listen to them pitching the U of I, you'd have thought it was Oxford.

"It's by far the best school in the state and one of the best in the country," one of them said. "It's known as the Harvard of the West."

He actually said that.

The invitation to join my friends there was appealing. It wasn't as if I had a lot of promising offers or anything pressing to do. I was at loose ends, wasn't close to settling on a career choice and missed playing music. My grades from my final semester at BJC were bad enough that the U of I wouldn't admit me until I repeated some classes I'd failed, but I could spend the spring semester playing in the band and enroll in summer school at BJC to retake the failed classes.

The University of Idaho is in Moscow, Idaho, 300 miles north of Boise. Getting there posed a problem. I'd sold my Volkswagen before leaving for the Navy. My friends would be driving back with their wives and babies and wouldn't have room for me in their small cars. The solution, such as it was, was a Greyhound bus.

The night before leaving, I set my suitcase on the floor on the left side of my bed and propped the Hofner guitar from Bremerhaven up against it. From such seemingly insignificant actions calamity can arise.

In ancient Rome, where the expression "getting up on the wrong side of the bed" originated, it was considered bad luck to get up on a bed's left side. For some reason, I did something I virtually never do and got up on the left side of the bed that morning. The room was still dark. I took one step and ran head-on into the guitar, landing on top of it with the sickening sounds of strings twanging and wood cracking. Switching on the light revealed the horror. The only guitar I owned at the time, and it was lying in two pieces on the bedroom floor, its neck snapped completely off.

What to do? The bus would be leaving soon, and with no guitar there was no point in going to Moscow.

"Just get on the bus," Mom said. "You already have your ticket. We'll drive you to the bus station and you can figure out how to get another guitar when you get to Moscow."

The bus ride was long and trying, with both sanity and hearing endangered by screaming babies, squealing toddlers, and rowdy college students. Driving to Moscow from Boise in good weather takes about six hours. By bus that January, it seemed to take forever. Then-Governor Cecil Andrus had dubbed the highway connecting North and South Idaho a "goat trail," and he wasn't far wrong. The two-lane road is narrow and winding, skirting whitewater rivers and climbing switchbacks. It was after dark when the bus pulled into Moscow.

Moscow was a different world from Boise. It wasn't just that it was a much smaller town, it also was doing a passable imitation of the Arctic. Boise had had maybe a couple of inches of thawing snow on the ground when the bus left that morning. Moscow had canyons of snow. They rose to face level or higher on both sides of sidewalks. The streets were glistening ribbons. Even the high temperatures were below zero. It reached 45 degrees below that winter, the hardest winter anyone there could remember. There were still patches of snow on the ground when we left in May. (The following winter, it rained so much that my parked car slid down a hill in an avalanche of mud, engulfed almost to its windows.)

A visit to a local music store yielded a cheap but serviceable guitar, and the band members already living in Moscow had found a place for me to stay. Within my modest means if I found a job quickly, it was a four-plex on a steep hillside. Two North Idaho students living in one of its four apartments were looking for someone to share the rent. I'd be living there with them and Vance, the keyboard player from the Mystics, who also been recruited to join the band and would be arriving later in the week.

Vance was nothing if not colorful, in a grungy-hippy sort of way. The students with whom we'd be sharing living space were serious students—clean-cut, wholesome college boys. It would have been difficult to find four people less suited to living together.

Vance and I shared a room with a bunk bed. The college students shared an identical bedroom. We pooled our money to pay for groceries, utilities, and other necessities, the most expensive being heat. It was so cold we permanently set the thermostat at 85 degrees and still shivered.

Finding a job wasn't difficult. *Playboy* magazine had given the University of Idaho the dubious honor of having the highest per-capita beer consumption of any college in the nation. Bartenders were always in demand, and it mattered little that I had no bartending experience. A tavern, The Alley, was owned by a man from Boise, and its manager and several bartenders were friends of the friends who had talked me into moving to Moscow. I was hired immediately.

It happened that The Alley also had a need for rock groups to play on weekends. We auditioned and more or less became the house band. I spent weekday afternoons behind the bar pouring beer and Friday and Saturday nights on the stage, playing current hits for the students who flocked there. The legal drinking age for beer in Idaho at the time was twenty. In neighboring Washington state, it was twenty-one. It followed that a tide of twenty-year-olds from Washington State University, seven miles away, migrated to the taverns of Moscow every weekend. The Alley was a teeming caldron of beer and hormones on Friday and Saturday nights, and we were at center stage.

One of my weekday tasks was opening the tavern for business. I'd get there a little after noon, unlock the door, turn on the lights and the Alley sign above the entrance, tap a keg if necessary and have everything ready to open at one o'clock. It was usually slow for the first hour or two. As the afternoon wore on and students finished classes for the day, it grew steadily busier.

Except for one memorable afternoon.

It was nearly two o'clock when the manager arrived that day.

"Hi, Tim," he said. "How's it going?"

"Pretty slow," I replied. "Actually, really slow. You're the first person to come through the door."

"Really? Well, I think it'll pick up soon."

Sure enough; within minutes, barstools were occupied, people were playing pool, and I was pouring beer steadily.

Our staff meetings were on Sunday afternoons, when the bar was closed. The manager waited till then to tell the staff about the day when business went from zero to normal in minutes.

"Tim was surprised at how quickly things picked up after I came in," he said. "Turns out he'd forgotten to turn on the sign and unlock the door."

We had a good laugh over that at my expense. The manager, incidentally, went on to become the chief executive officer of the J. R. Simplot Co., which its billionaire namesake had built into Idaho's largest privately held company. Among other things, it supplied the potatoes used to make McDonald's french fries. Many years later, I interviewed my former boss for a *Statesman* story while he was serving in that capacity. We both had a chuckle reminiscing about the slow day at The Alley.

The fledgling band rehearsed whenever there was time in everyone's schedules. My schedule wasn't a problem, as I only worked afternoons, and Vance's days consisted primarily of watching television and drinking beer. We rehearsed whenever the students of the group got a break from classes, studying and the demands of their home lives, usually once or twice a week. Rehearsals were held at the house where our drummer and his wife lived. We learned songs by Creedence Clearwater Revival, Cream, Jimi Hendrix, Three Dog Night, Deep Purple, The Beatles, Rolling Stones, Guess Who, and other groups popular at the time. We named the band "Hope." We weren't particularly good—we didn't have the time or the motivation to practice as much as the Mystics did—but we were popular. The Alley was almost always packed on the nights we played.

We played for fraternity and sorority house parties as well. We were playing at a fraternity house the first time we did Three Dog Night's "Joy to the World," then a hit song that we had no business even attempting. Only two members of the group sang, making Three Dog Night's signature three-part vocal harmonies impossible, and neither of us had voices as good as theirs. Our rendition of the song started tentatively, grew swiftly worse, then fell apart entirely—one instrument at a time. The last to stop playing was the drummer, and then only after banging away for several seconds before realizing he was playing all by himself. It was humiliating enough without the acid comment made by a fraternity brother sitting at a table inches from the stage.

"Wow! That sounded just like Three Dog Night!"

That spring, a fraternity hired us to play at a barn dance. A makeshift stage had been set up for us on the barn's second floor. It was clean and tidy, as barns go, but a permeating smell hinted of trouble.

"Is that horses we're smelling?" I asked the barn's owner as we were setting up our gear the afternoon before the party. "I don't see any, but it smells like horses. Are there horses around here somewhere?"

"Sure are," he proudly replied. "There's sixty of them downstairs."

It happens that I am Allergic to horses. Upper Case Allergic. Concerned about her son's continual sniffling and sneezing, my mother took me to an allergist when I was a preschooler. A nurse gave me the usual test, allergen serums in scratches she'd made on my back, waited the prescribed amount of time and, in some alarm, summoned the doctor.

The doc took one look at my back and solemnly addressed my mother. I remember his words:

"Mrs. Woodward, our scale goes from one to four, but to horses your son is about a seven."

Getting anywhere near a horse gives me asthma. If the exposure lasts long enough, my eyes swell shut.

So you can understand my reaction upon learning that sixty horses were milling about a few feet beneath my feet.

"Sorry, guys. I can't play tonight. You'll have to find somebody to fill in for me."

"Can't play? Are you nuts? Why not?"

"Horses, that's why. I'm deathly allergic to them. I'll barely be able to see or breathe, let along sing and play."

After a long, uncomfortable silence, the barn's owner proposed a solution.

"I have a barn heater," he said. "It blows a stream of hot air. We could set it up in front of the band and point it at you while you're playing. The hot air would blow the allergens away from you."

It sounded iffy, but we didn't have a lot of options. We'd signed a contract to play, several hundred people would show up expecting us to play, and it would have been virtually impossible to find someone on a few hours' notice to fill in for me.

When we returned that evening, resplendent in flowered shirts and bell-bottom pants, the barn heater had been set up in front of my spot on the stage. When we started to play, its owner fired it up. The blast of hot air might as well have come from the hubs of hell.

It seemed to work, though. We made it through several songs without my eyes or lungs going on strike.

The other band members, however, were cracking up.

"What's so funny?"

They were laughing so hard that at first they couldn't answer. When the laughter subsided a bit, one of them told me to go look in a mirror when we took our break.

The nearest one was the rearview mirror in my car. The reflection looking back from it was soon laughing as hard as the other band members had. The barn heater had singed the tips of my brown hair, eyebrows, sideburns, and mustache snow white.

As the spring semester passed and Vance and I became increasingly settled in our routine, the serious students with whom we shared the apartment became increasingly unsettled about us. And not without reason. There was the music, of course (we often played records, both for enjoyment and to learn new songs), which wasn't conducive to their studying. There were love interests, mostly Vance's, who came and went at all hours. Neither of the students had girlfriends, so this may have rubbed them the wrong way in more ways than one.

And of course there was Vance himself.

Vance was short and balding, with long, wispy hair in the places where it hadn't disappeared. He often looked as if he'd slept in his clothes, which he occasionally did, but he had a good heart and could be funny in a uniquely Vance sort of way. Inspired by a photo on an album cover, in which Eric Clapton and the other members of his band were dressed in silver satin suits, he bought a cheap pair of slacks and a jacket at a thrift store, sprayed-painted them silver, and wore them to one of our gigs. The fumes almost asphyxiated us, but it was impossible not to laugh.

Vance's personal life was a train wreck. More than once he would wake up in the morning, still wearing his clothes from the day before, have a beer for breakfast, and leave to begin his day. What he did all day when he wasn't at the apartment was a mystery—he never did enroll at the university—but whatever it was sealed his reputation as a deadbeat.

The four of us were having dinner one night when a knock at the door almost broke it down.

"Tell them I'm not here," Vance said, grabbing a slice of pizza and scurrying down the hall to lock himself in the bathroom.

"May I help you?" one of our house mates asked a burly young man glowering on the porch, looking as if he wanted to break someone's legs.

"Vance here?" he asked.

"Vance? Uh … I think he just left."

"Tell him I'm looking for him. If he doesn't pay by the time I find him he's not going to like it."

Only after the bill collector had been gone for several minutes did Vance emerge from the bathroom, holding a wilting slice of pizza and looking queasy.

"Sorry about that," he said.

"What was that all about, Vance? The guy looked like he was ready to kill you."

"Well … I owe some people money."

"What people?"

"Well … the Rathskeller for one."

The Rathskeller was a pizza parlor where he briefly worked and apparently had run up an impressive tab.

"Okay, that's one. Where else?"

"Well, there's the music store where I bought my foot pedal."

"On credit?"

"I paid them a little bit. But I still owe on it."

The foot pedal was a device to control the volume on his keyboard. He liked it so much he'd nicknamed one of his girlfriends "Foot Pedal." She was a pretty girl, the only one of his girlfriends who was both pretty and slender. Vance had a predilection for plain and plump.

"Who else do you owe?" we asked him.

"Look, it's not a big deal. Just forget it, okay? And if anyone else comes around looking for me, I'm not here."

Vance's mode of transportation was a rundown 1963 Pontiac the size of a small whale. Surpassingly ugly, it had the redeeming features of a commodious back seat and a cavernous trunk that made it perfect for hauling band equipment. We had to tear down and move our gear out of The Alley after playing there Saturday nights, and the biggest portion of it ended up in Vance's car. On a bitterly cold night, the

Pontiac played the leading role in one of Vance's ongoing misadventures.

It was somewhere around two o'clock in the morning when we got back to the apartment after our gig. We were too tired to unload the gear so we left it in the car, planning to unload it in the morning. The Pontiac, parked facing downhill on the icy street, was poised for mayhem.

Early Sunday morning, we awoke to yet another furious knock on the door. This was not unusual; we'd almost come to expect it. It was unusual, however, for it to happen so early in the morning, especially on a Sunday.

Vance actually answered the door this time.

"Are you the owner of that ugly blue Pontiac?"

"Who wants to know?"

"Me, that's who!"

"Who are you?"

"I'm your neighbor down the street. Do you want to know why I want to know who owns that ugly blue car?"

"Uh, yeah … I guess."

"Take a look down the hill."

Vance gingerly ventured into the icy morning, dressed only in his skivvies and a Jimi Hendrix T-shirt.

"Is that yours?" the man asked, pointing at a car that had slid down the street and into a driveway at the bottom of the hill.

Not even Vance could think of a way to deny it.

"It does look like it," he admitted.

The Pontiac, all two tons of it plus an additional half-ton of band equipment, had succumbed to gravity on the slick street in the dead of night, hurtling down the hillside like an armed torpedo and virtually demolishing the indignant neighbor's small economy car.

To this day, I don't know what the outcome was. The neighbor undoubtedly filed a claim. Vance may or may not have had insurance; my guess is the latter. If the neighbor took him to court, I never heard about it. Vance could be tight-lipped about such things, and he was uncommonly good at wriggling his way out of tight spots. I never asked him about it, knowing the answer would be suspect if there even was an answer. I knew him from high school until his passing from a terminal case of beer drinking many years later, and much about him still remains a mystery.

Vance and I were unusual among people our age in not being students in a university town teeming with them. When the spring semester ended, I returned to Boise to retake the two BJC classes I'd failed in hopes of being admitted to the university in the fall.

A Boise friend, Keith Kiler, finished his hitch in the Navy that summer, and we celebrated by going fishing. An avid angler, Keith chose as our destination the world famous Silver Creek, near Sun Valley. Silver Creek had been a favorite trout stream of Ernest Hemingway, Gary Cooper, and other celebrities and is known for its highly educated trout. We fished all day and caught nothing, but kept our spirits up by drinking prodigious quantities of beer.

Weary of our best offerings being snubbed by finicky fish, we called it a day and drove to Sun Valley in hopes of spotting a celebrity or two. By then it was dark. I was driving.

"Turn here," Keith said as we were passing the Sun Valley Lodge.

What he meant was for me to turn onto a road a hundred feet or so ahead of us. Misinterpreting his intent, beer undoubtedly being a contributing factor, I took an immediate hard right.

In what seemed like seconds, we were soaking wet and surrounded by flashing lights on police cars. This was understandable, considering that my Volkswagen was half submerged in the lily pond in front of the lodge.

It was the Saturday of Memorial Day weekend. We spent three long nights and two longer days in the Ketchum jail, waiting for a judge to return to work on Tuesday and hear our case. The daytime temperatures outside were in the nineties. In our cell, it was hotter. Whether by design or a mechanical problem, the jail's radiators were going full blast.

The judge was a jolly, conspiratorial sort.

"So, you boys were celebrating getting out of the Navy, eh?"

"Yes, your honor."

He winked.

"I was in the Navy, too."

A hopeful sign.

He studied our file briefly before rendering his decision.

"I'm fining you boys each five dollars plus two dollars and fifty cents court costs."

He winked again.

"And I'll make sure this never gets in your records in Boise."

We were beyond grateful. In hindsight, however, he should at the very least have given us a meaningful fine and suspended our licenses for a while. Who knows how many drunk drivers have killed people because lenient judges winked and set them free? That's changed since then, and rightly so.

It was my good fortune that summer to join a group with the most naturally gifted musician I ever knew. His name was Leo Lawrence. Short and slightly built with blue eyes and towhead-blond hair, he reminded me of a leprechaun. In addition to being a gifted songwriter, Leo had the voice of an angel, a genius for playing rhythm guitar, and perfect pitch.

Perfect pitch is the ability to identify a note simply by hearing it. It's said to exist in one to five people out of every 10,000. Often those people have musical training early in childhood. Leo was the son of a blind piano tuner. He grew up listening to tones his father played while tuning pianos. We used to joke that you could burp and Leo would tell you what note it was. He learned songs effortlessly, playing them perfectly after hearing them a single time.

The band we started with him that summer was named Calico. The most popular group in the country at the time was Crosby, Stills, Nash, and Young, known for their tight vocal harmonies. The band minus Leo spent hours practicing a particularly challenging song on one of their albums. We tried to learn it without him because we knew it would take a while for the rest of us but that he'd pick it up immediately.

In this we were not disappointed. Not only did he play his guitar part perfectly on the first hearing, he claimed to hear not four but seven vocal parts, identified the four most important ones, and taught each of us our parts. When we sang it together, it sounded so much like CSN&Y that we broke out laughing.

Leo came to a tragic end. At rehearsals, in his little pink house on Broadway Avenue, he routinely drank half a pint of whisky and several beers without ever appearing to be drunk. He died several years after Calico disbanded, crashing his car into a bridge abutment on Christmas Eve. All that talent, all the wonderful music he could have made with it, gone at the age of twenty-nine.

One of the failed courses I repeated at BJC that summer was, ironically, music appreciation. What the other was I've forgotten. My grades in them during summer school were good enough to raise my grade point average enough to be admitted to the Harvard of the West.

One thing the university actually did have in common with Harvard was less-than-championship-caliber athletic teams. My introduction to the Vandal football team came in a preseason television interview with its coach.

"Well, coach, you're playing the University of Texas El Paso this weekend," the announcer said. "Last year UTEP beat the Vandals sixty to nothing. How do you see this year's game shaping up?"

"Well, I'll tell you one thing," the coach answered. "It's not going to be sixty to nothing."

He was right. It was 60-3.

I attended one game that year. The Vandals were playing at nearby Washington State University's stadium because their old wooden stadium had burned down the year before. Rumor had it that students had deliberately set the fire. I didn't put much stock in the rumor until actually attending a Vandal game. Students were throwing empty wine bottles at the players on the bench. Not the opposing team's players, *their own players*. I was shocked, and even more shocked when someone yelled "duck" a couple of heartbeats before a flaming cardboard box flew over my head. Students in the upper rows were setting boxes ablaze and throwing them at the fans below. The object was to bat the box away from you in such a way that it continued its descent all the way to the field. My date and I left the game early, having had enough of this sport. It was the last Vandal football game I would attend for many years. If the U of I wanted me to become a Vandal fan—I'd been a Boise Junior College Bronco fan since childhood—this was not the way to go about it.

Still not having made a career choice, I opted to major in architecture. My father had an abiding interest in any new building that was being built in downtown Boise, an interest he passed on to me. Designing buildings struck me as a pleasantly productive way to spend one's working years.

True, perhaps, if you're a left-brained, analytical person. Decidedly right-brained, I might as well have majored in nuclear physics. It took one semester to realize that, appealing as it sounded, architecture wasn't for me.

Next was advertising, which I saw as a way to be creative and still make a good living. Dad had encouraged me from an early age to become a doctor or a lawyer, professions which, as a self-made man who never finished high school, he saw as the epitome of success. Advertising was a middle ground. I figured that I could satisfy my creative side by dreaming up catchy jingles and slogans and still have a nice house with a BMW in the garage. Dad would be pleased, and it could be an okay life.

One year as an advertising major was enough to sink that theory. It wasn't just that the classes failed to motivate me. The nail in the advertising coffin was an issue of a trade magazine in which advertising executives invariably were shown wearing suits and ties, cocktails in hand, at events celebrating their success. The posed, stilted-looking photos all looked the same. Only the faces were different. This was not my idea of success, or how I wanted to spend my life.

The summer before my senior year, I made one of the best decisions of my life. I was home in Boise, sitting at Dad's desk at the time, working up the courage to call my advisor on Dad's phone. After months of soul searching, I decided it was more important to be happy, to do what you enjoy and think you'd be good at, than it is to make a lot of money.

You know in your heart when a decision is sound. This one was. Feeling better about college than I had in months, I called Dr. Bert Cross, my advisor and head of the university's journalism school. The school at that time had three options as majors: advertising, radio and television, and news-editorial. Balding with a kindly face and a fondness for bow ties, Dr. Cross was a good advisor, a good man.

"Hello, Dr. Cross?"

"Yes?"

"This is Tim Woodward."

"Hi, Tim. How are things down there in Boise?"

"Fine, thanks. Dr. Cross, I've been wondering about something."

"Oh? What's that?"

"Is it too late to change my major to news-editorial?"

There was a sharp intake of air. Not quite a gasp, but not far from it. Then, a protracted silence.

"… Tim?"

"Yes?"

"Nobody changes majors when they're a senior."

Convinced that I was serious, he worked it out so that I could. It would mean taking some twenty credits in each of my last semesters, but it could be done.

In August, I returned to Moscow to look for a place to live before school started. A gas war was being waged at the time, and I was shocked upon pulling into a service station to see the lowest price per gallon I had ever seen or ever would see—just under a quarter per gallon. Commenting on it to the attendant who filled my tank, I was stunned by his response.

"It's been this low all summer," he said. "We jack it up again when the students come back."

The place I found to live was a basement apartment in the home of an elderly couple. It was small and gloomy, but the price was right—fifty bucks a month. And with some paint, brightly colored curtains on its only window, and some posters and pictures on the walls, it was almost cozy. I settled in and prepared to attack a demanding senior year.

One of the most important lessons the Navy had taught me was the importance of working hard to get what you want in life. As much as I enjoyed the travel, the work and the friends made in the Navy, its regimentation and obsession with hair-splitting regulations made me devoutly committed to learning skills that would spare me a lifetime of that sort of thing. That and finally having a college major that seemed to make sense combined to make me a serious student.

As I'd already taken a year of German to fulfill the two-year foreign language requirement, more German was part of that senior year, along with economics, business law, Law of the Press, Ethics of the Press, and other journalism courses, and what passed for typography. The press used for the typography class looked like a hand-me-down from Gutenberg himself. The type was set by hand, a single letter a time. Pressure was applied to the inked letters against paper with a massive iron wheel turned by hand.

It looked medieval, but with enough time and patience one could actually print something on it. No one would have dreamed of using it to print anything as lengthy as a newspaper story, but it worked well enough to make a fake press card. The impetus for this was a sold-out Neil Diamond concert at Washington State University. The girl I was dating at the time wanted to go, and, though not a fan of Diamond, I liked some of his songs well enough that I wanted to go, too.

Tickets were impossible to get, which was where the ancient printing press came in handy. Following the instructions learned in typography class, I made marginally believable *Lewiston Tribune* press cards. The *Tribune* was the largest newspaper in that part of Idaho. On the night of the concert, my girlfriend and I presented our *Tribune* press cards at the door. I was armed with a camera; she was carrying a reporter's notebook. The ticket taker eyed the cards briefly and let us pass. Delighted and feeling smug with our success, we settled into some empty seats near the top row of the gymnasium and proceeded to enjoy the concert. As Diamond was playing his encore song, my date had an idea.

"Let's see if we can go interview him," she said. "See that line of real press people standing down there by the stage. We have our press cards. Let's go down there and join them."

The plan was not without flaws, the main one being that the legitimate press people waiting in the line all knew each other. I was pretty certain that a couple of college "journalists" sidling up to them would arouse suspicion, an expectation that did not go unfulfilled.

"What are you shooting?" one of the photographers asked me.

"What? Oh, uh … black and white."

"Ah," he said, trying not to laugh.

"Who are you with?"

"*The Lewiston Tribune.*"

A knot had formed in my stomach and I was beginning to sweat, symptoms of anxiety that increased upon noticing his press ID. He *was* with the *Lewiston Tribune.*

To his credit, he didn't rat us out. He merely nodded and smiled, most likely amused by our audacity. The other legitimate journalists were staring at us and smiling, too. We clearly had been exposed, but none of them said a word. They seemed to be enjoying it.

Before one or both of us could succumb to a panic attack, the real journalists and the two imposters were ushered down a hall and through a door to a parking lot behind the gym.

"Mr. Diamond will meet you here," we were told.

It was a windy, bitterly cold night. We stood there shivering for maybe ten minutes. Then, a black limousine approached. It stopped beside us, inches away. A power window rolled down, and there, close enough to touch, was Neil Diamond. He looked right at us.

"Great concert, Neil," one of the reporters said. "Can we ask you a few questions?"

A long pause. Then the power window rolled back up and the limousine began to move, leaving us shivering in a cloud of exhaust, watching the taillights grow smaller and disappear. Diamond never said a word.

"What a jerk!" one of the reporters said, to universal agreement.

I haven't been able to listen to a Neil Diamond song since without thinking the same thing.

This, regrettably, was about as close as I came during my time at the U of I to learning any of the practical skills needed to be a working journalist. Most of our time in class was spent discussing lofty theories or current events. We visited a real newspaper only once. We didn't have to cover a student council meeting, a city council or school board meeting, a police or courts story, write an editorial, or do almost any of the other things journalists do on a daily basis. My only assignment to write something for the student newspaper resulted in a column about local merchants gouging students (raising gas prices when we returned in the fall being a notable example). Some of the local merchants responded by canceling their advertising. That, at least, was a realistic newspaper experience.

The journalism faculty consisted of three teachers—the kindly, avuncular Dr. Cross, a teacher named Ralph, and another teacher named Jim Van Leuven. Dr. Cross was a competent and beloved teacher. Ralph tried hard, but was not a born teacher. Jim was. He was smart, fiery, and inspired in us a passion for our craft. He also was the source of one of my favorite newspaper stories.

Jim had once worked for a newspaper in a small town in Washington state, so small that the departure of a local minister and the announcement of his replacement were front-page news. The town had been without a minister long enough that it was the lead story on Page One, accompanied by a photograph of the new minister and his family. I've forgotten his name, but let's say it was Smith. The cutline under the photo was supposed to have read, "Pictured are the Reverend Smith, his wife, and their two sons."

Except for a typo that had the ruinous effect of changing "sons" to "sins."

Newspaper lore is rife with such stories. A coworker who had worked at a paper in Tennessee delighted in telling a story about a recipe that was supposed to have called for two cups of chopped celery but instead advised readers to use two cups of "chopped clergy." A headline for a *Statesman* story reporting a record turnout for a Veterans Day football game read, "10,000 Participate in VD Activities." A course listing in *The Statesman* was supposed to have read, "Managing Your Hard Disk," but the "s" became a "c."

Though they may not have given us a lot in the way of hands-on experience, Jim and Dr. Cross taught us pretty much everything else we needed to know and inspired us to work toward becoming the best journalists we could be. They made us appreciate the importance of journalism's sacred trust to inform the public, the reason the founding fathers protected it in the First Amendment to the Constitution. They lit a fire under us.

Thanks in no small part to that and the fire kindled by my service in the Navy, I got straight As at the U of I with the exception of a course in which I had zero interest and took only because it fit my schedule and fulfilled a requirement. The course was Economic Geography. I got a B.

I'd just taken the final exam for it when a friend who also was in the class made a troubling observation. I'd been feeling a bit under the weather for several days. When we ran into each other in a hallway after the final, his eyes grew wide.

"Are you okay?" he asked.

"No. I don't feel very good."

"Go look in a mirror," he said.

Staring back at me from a men's room mirror was a face dotted with red spots.

"What seems to be the problem?" the ancient doctor at the Student Health Center asked.

"Well, I haven't been feeling well for a few days, and now I have these spots on my face."

"Spots? What spots?"

"The ones on my face! You don't see them?"

With this he shuffled to the door and turned on an overhead light. Then he switched on a light he was wearing on his forehead.

"Well, I'll be! Nurse! Nurse, get in here! This boy's got the schmeasles."

I did, in fact, have the schmeasles, just in time for semester break. I spent it at my folks' home in Boise, recuperating in time to return for the spring semester.

One of my nonjournalism teachers rivaled the student health center doctor in years and had the wisdom one might expect from someone of his advanced age. He taught, among other things, Business Law. I'll never forget his answer to a student who asked him whether he thought BJC would ever be as big as the U of I.

"All I can tell you," the venerable professor replied, "is that you cannot long keep the centers of education away from the centers of population."

Then a junior college, Boise State now offers masters and doctoral programs, is home to the state's only engineering school, annually fields one of the nation's top football teams, is the state's largest university, and "a metropolitan research university." The wise old professor seemed to see all that coming.

I seriously dated several girls during my time at the U of I, one from Boise, a Washington State student from Seattle, and another WSU student from Olympia, Washington. The last I met during a break when my group was playing at The Alley. She talked for pretty much the whole break. When I excused myself because it was time to go play again, she apologized for not letting me get a word in edgewise.

"That's okay," I truthfully replied. "I like to listen (a good trait for a journalist)."

I've often joked that that was when she knew I was the man for her. This was the same girl who had inspired me to make fake press cards to go to the Neil Diamond concert. A girl with whom I suspected life would never be boring.

And my future wife. Life with Sheila did, in fact, turn out to be anything but dull. She's whip smart, an adventurous spirit, a gifted conversationalist, and one of the most generous people I've ever known.

We graduated in May. After all but flunking out at BJC, I graduated with honors from the U of I.

And never did receive a diploma. It was withheld because of unpaid campus parking tickets and a library fine, which together might have totaled twenty bucks.

Not that I lost sleep over it. A wedding and the trip of a lifetime lay ahead.

CHAPTER SIX
Newlyweds

Early in our courtship, my future wife and I discovered that we both had signed up for a trip jointly offered by the University of Idaho and Washington State University, where she graduated the same week I received my diploma, theoretically speaking, from the U of I.

The price of the trip seemed almost too good to be true. For less than $300, students and members of their families could take a round-trip flight from Seattle to Amsterdam and spend the summer in Europe. The price included dinner and hotel accommodations upon arrival in Amsterdam and dinner and a second night's accommodations the night before the flight back to Seattle ten weeks later. We were thrilled to learn that we could spend the summer in Europe together.

My parents couldn't believe what a good deal it was. Such a good deal that, to my astonishment, they said they might be interested in going themselves. Their interest in leaving home for a summer was so out of character as to be almost beyond belief. My parents rarely traveled anywhere.

In all the years, I could remember them taking only three trips together. In 1955, they took the train to Flint, Michigan, to pick up the new Buick Dad had ordered. In my teenage years, they surprised me by saying they were confident leaving me alone to keep an eye on things while they drove to San Francisco for a rare vacation that ended on its first day. Dad drove the Buick into a cow outside of Jordan Valley, Oregon, cutting the trip short and ruining my plans for a party of shocking proportions. The only time they had been out of the United States was a trip they had taken with wacky Uncle Bill and Aunt Mary to Mexico and Guatemala, searching for a safe haven to escape the Communist takeover Uncle Bill never tired of predicting. They came home disillusioned and vowing not to leave home again for a long time, if ever. The possibility of them going to Europe for an entire summer seemed almost surreal.

They signed up almost immediately, an alarming turn of events. Knowing it would lead to a living-in-sin lecture, I hadn't told them that Sheila was going.

"My parents are going!" I told Sheila. "What are we going to do? You know how conservative they are."

"Maybe we could sit far away from each other on the plane," she suggested. "I could wear a blonde wig and they wouldn't recognize me. I could hang out with

Sheila Woodward, mid-1970s.

a friend who's going, and you could spend a few days with your mom and dad in Amsterdam and then tell them you decided to head out on your own with a buddy."

We considered this option for as long as it took to realize that, in addition to the distasteful aspect of lying to my parents, we were almost certain to be found out sooner or later, most likely sooner.

Another option, though it would be a bit rushed, didn't involve lying.

We could get married. The wedding was in the church Sheila's family attended in Olympia, Washington. Sheila looked stunning with her dark hair and summer tan contrasting with her wedding dress. I wore a tuxedo copied from the one Beatle George Harrison had worn for his wedding. The burly priest who married us had once played for the Green Bay Packers, and how many priests can say that?

The wedding was characterized by the sort of minor debacles that would eventually provide fodder for my newspaper columns. Sheila's then brother-in-law was in charge of the music. We should have known better, as he was something of a know-it-all who couldn't be trusted to stick to the plan. At the point where he was supposed to have played a recording of a song, there was a long, awkward silence. In a poignant part of the ceremony where no song should have been, everyone was caught off guard by disruptive music booming through the speakers. When members of the wedding party were invited to offer a prayer for the bride and groom, Sheila's brother mumbled something that was mistaken for the last thing anyone wanted to hear. We never knew what he actually said, but it gave the impression that the marriage would be over almost before it began.

"Divorce? Did he say they were getting a divorce?"

"They're getting a divorce already? They aren't even married yet!"

At the reception, I mistook a distant aunt and uncle for some long-unseen friends of my parents.

"Hello, Tim," they said as they reached the front of the reception line. "Congratulations to you and Sheila."

"I remember you! Ivan and Billie Sager, right? Nice to see you again."

A long pause.

"No … we're your Aunt Edward and Uncle Nita."

The party after the reception at the church was at Sheila's parents' house, where it became obvious that her brother-in-law wasn't the only poor choice of helpers. Sheila's mother had asked a neighbor named Jerry to serve as bartender. It was a logical if misguided choice, seeing how Jerry was a hopeless lush. When my mother, who was close to being a teetotaler, asked him for a drink, Jerry was happy to oblige. She was probably thinking something along the lines of the fruity, Annie Green Springs wine she occasionally drank at home. Jerry was thinking more along the lines of boilermakers. Within half an hour, Mom was staggering, slurring her words, and embarrassed as she had ever been. Sheila's folks carried her upstairs and put her to bed. For the rest or her life, she blushed whenever anyone mentioned it.

We had a couple of nights before the flight was to leave for Amsterdam and planned to spend our wedding night at Ocean Shores, a short drive away on the Washington coast. Sheila's father loaned us his station wagon to drive there. We had to stop for something on our way out of Olympia, and for the life of me I couldn't get the car back in gear again. Married for roughly four hours, we had to call home for help.

We were glad we decided to get married rather than using the blonde-wig option on the flight because it allowed us to sit with my folks and share the excitement of heading to glamorous European destinations for the summer. Our plan was to buy a car in Amsterdam and drive from there to Germany. Mom, never at a loss for something memorable to say, provided the most memorable moment of the flight with an observation about the tourist German she'd been studying.

"I don't see why the Germans say 'guten tag,'" she said.

"It's their way of saying hello," I said, glad for the chance to show off my two years of college German. "It means good day."

"Why don't they just say hello?" Mom asked.

"That is their way of saying hello. We say hello. They said good day."

"But if they mean hello, why don't they say hello? Why beat around the bush with all this 'guten tag' business?"

Sheila could be forgiven for wondering what sort of family she'd married into.

Amsterdam was, well, Amsterdam—picturesque, charming, uniquely beautiful. We spent part of our time there enjoying the museums, the tulips and chocolates, and the rest of the time looking for the car that would carry us around Europe. I'd sold my Volkswagen before leaving home. My heart was set on a used BMW, which I naively assumed could be purchased quickly and cheaply in Germany, where BMWs are made. The four us took the train to Munich, where the search for a car would begin.

One of our first stops was Munich's Hofbrau Haus, famed for its beer. A waitress who could have posed for a painting of a stereotypical, dirndl-clad beer maid brought us huge mugs of the best beer any of us had ever had. Dad, who rarely drank because of his diabetes, was the most congenial I ever saw him. His face was flushed, his eyes bloodshot, but his normal reserve vanished. He joked, laughed, sang. He undoubtedly paid for it the next morning, but it may well have been one of the most convivial nights of his life.

Mom, on the other hand, was miserable in Munich. She hated the language barrier, the hotel where we were staying, the continental breakfasts.

"Why can't they speak English and give us bacon and eggs once in a while?"

Mostly, she hated the rain.

"Doesn't it ever stop raining here? It's supposed to be summer."

One morning she pushed her continental breakfast aside, abruptly stood up and announced that she was leaving.

"Where are you going?"

"Home," she replied.

With that she exited the hotel and stormed down the street to God knew where.

"Mom!" I shouted as we ran after her. "What do you think you're doing?"

"I'm getting out of here."

"You're going home?"

"Yes."

"How? You don't have a plane ticket. You don't speak the language. You don't even have your suitcase or your passport."

Minor details she hadn't considered. We were able to talk her back to the hotel, where she reluctantly agreed to give Europe another try. If the rain didn't stop soon, however, she said she would be on the next plane home, with or without the rest of us.

The search for a BMW was neither fruitful nor pleasant. While Mom and Dad took in the sights of Munich—the weather had gotten sunnier and with it her disposition—Sheila and I scanned classified ads in newspapers and took streetcars and taxis to distant parts of the city to look at cars that were either too old and unreliable or too expensive.

It took a week to find one that was neither. An American soldier stationed in Munich was selling it because he was about to be discharged. It was the model I wanted, it was in good condition and the price was fair. All we had to do was have it pass a U.S. Army inspection and a German government inspection, which was a little like saying all we had to do was buy lederhosen and join an oompah band.

The army paperwork required us to take a train to Heidelberg, some four hours away, to have official forms completed. Then it was back to Munich for the German auto inspection. That done, we'd be on our way. A German auto inspection, however, is to an American auto inspection what chess is to tiddlywinks. The car was all but disassembled, with individual parts inspected both by human eyes and electronic equipment. The car came achingly close to passing. Everything was perfect except for one of the brakes. To pass the inspection, the brakes would have to be rebuilt, requiring time and money we couldn't afford. We already had spent the better part of two weeks in Munich searching for my dream Beemer.

"I've had it with this!" Sheila said. "Let's go back to that place we saw at the

Amsterdam airport and buy a new car to ship home at the end of the summer. We could get a new one for what a used BMW would cost here, and it would have a warranty."

She had a point. Leaving my folks in Munich, we returned to Amsterdam by train. The next day, we were in a gleaming showroom debating between two new cars. One was a baby blue Volkswagen bug. I had owned several VWs at home and had nothing but good luck with them. Parked next to it was a cherry red Fiat 850 Sport Coupe.

"That one's really pretty," Sheila said.

"It sure is. Looks like it would be a lot of fun to drive, too."

That said, I recalled a college buddy joking that the word Fiat was an acronym for "Fix it Again, Tony."

"I wonder if it would be a mistake, though. It's sporty and all, but what if it's a lemon? I've heard that Fiats aren't very reliable."

"If that's true, then we should get the VW. We know they're reliable."

"On the other hand, it's a brand-new Fiat with a warranty. And we only have two months left in Europe, and part of it will be in Italy—where Fiats are made. How much could go wrong in two months?"

We bought it and arranged to have it shipped to Seattle at the end of the summer. I hadn't had a sports car since my very first car, an MG that cost as much to keep running for a year as it did to purchase, and had forgotten how much fun they are to drive. It was a joy to run through the Fiat's gears, and it cornered like it was glued to the road.

The next day, we drove to a campground where we spent the night. (A summer's worth of hotel bills wasn't in our budget, so we'd purchased a tent and sleeping bags.) We were sitting by a campfire, celebrating the purchase of our new car and the prospect of an idyllic summer on the open road when we noticed something gleaming in the firelight from the Fiat's back tires. Closer inspection proved it to be steel belts protruding through what was left of their rubber.

"The tires are shot? After one day of driving? I don't believe it!"

"They must be defective."

"No kidding!"

"Well, we have the warranty papers. We'll just take it to a Fiat dealer and they'll replace the tires for free."

The campground was in a sparsely populated part of Germany. Finding a Fiat dealer there was about as likely as finding a Democrat in the Idaho Legislature. We wasted a day looking for one before springing for new rear tires. Oddly, the front tires still looked new.

The second set of rear tires lasted longer, but not very much. The mechanic who replaced them explained that the rear tires on that model of Fiat had to be aligned. Most cars only need to have their front tires aligned, usually after a front-end accident or a hard bump against a curbing. The rear tires on our car had to be aligned after negotiating a puddle or grazing a tumbleweed. We went through more rear tires that summer than I've purchased since or expect to purchase for the rest of my life.

It was one thing after another with that car. Successive batteries burned themselves out of distilled water and died in acrid-smelling clouds of smoke. Service station attendants didn't get it when we asked them to check the gas and fill up the battery.

We were driving down a road in France when a side rearview mirror fell off and shattered.

All this in a car that was barely a month old.

It did get us where we wanted to go, though, in addition to providing spending money for mechanics in multiple countries. The only place where we couldn't get the car fixed was Italy.

"What's wrong with it?" an Italian mechanic asked us.

"The batteries keep burning up."

"Take it to Germany. That's where all the good mechanics are."

We did take it to Germany and, over the course of the summer, some twenty other countries. The finicky Fiat notwithstanding, it was one of the best summers of our lives. We "oohed" and "awed" over paintings in the Louvre, picnicked in the shadow of the Matterhorn, shopped in the public market in Tangier. Great memories.

Two unpleasant memories, however, remain the most vivid.

One was getting sick in Greece. We'd been driving for hours in withering heat, gotten lost, and paid one exorbitant toll-road fee after another by the time we arrived in a small, seaside town in northern Greece. We were hot, tired, grumpy, and sick of driving. One look at Kamena Vourla's idyllic campground on the shores of the Adriatic and we decided to stop and stay for as long as it took to feel like climbing back into the car again. We spent the better part of two weeks there, swimming in the clear blue sea, reading books, living on fresh fruits and vegetables, hearty breads, gyro sandwiches, and retsina wine. Almost everything was inexpensive in Europe then—you really could live there on five dollars a day—but in Greece things were sublimely cheap. Gyros cost the equivalent of nine cents. Fruits and vegetables were pennies a bag. We befriended an elderly Australian couple at the campground and enjoyed wonderful meals of fresh fruits and vegetables and freshly baked breads with them.

A sandwich purchased from a vendor in town, however, made me as sick as I've ever been. I had to visit the campground's outhouse every fifteen or twenty minutes, day and night. It would have been bad enough at home in a comfortable bed, but stuck in a sweltering tent on an air mattress it was beyond miserable. I was flat-on-my-back sick for the better part of a week.

To get to Greece, we'd had to drive through Yugoslavia. Yugoslavia, which broke apart after a series of political upheavals in the 1990s, was at the time made up of Bosnia and Herzegovina, Croatia, Macedonia, Montenegro, Serbia, and Slovenia. It was a hardline Communist country, neither a happy place nor a welcoming one.

On mountain passes, we repeatedly got stuck behind khaki-colored army trucks belching diesel fumes. The roads had so many twists and turns that it took a long time to reach stretches straight enough to pass. More than once, drivers of the trucks used arm signals to indicate that the way ahead was clear when it wasn't. Only when we pulled out from behind the trucks into the oncoming lane were we able to see vehicles heading straight for us and narrowly avoid collisions.

People working in fields threw rocks at us as we passed. At railroad crossings, boys threw muddy water on our windshield and demanded to be paid for "cleaning" it.

The strangest incident happened in Skopje, a city in northern Macedonia. Directional signs were rarities in Yugoslavia; we were lost about half of the time. We pulled into Skopje's town square to look for a sign with directions to the next town, and ultimately to Greece because we couldn't get out of Yugoslavia fast enough. The square was utterly deserted. Skopje was a city of nearly half a million people, and in midafternoon on the square's broad expanse were zero signs of life. No old men lounging on benches, no mothers pushing baby carriages, no flirting teenagers—absolutely no one. It was eerie.

We were looking for a sign with directions when a door opened in one of the buildings on the edge of the square and a mob ran out. Hundreds of angry, screaming people—all of them heading directly for … us.

They surrounded the car, picked it up, rocked it.

"This is it!" Sheila said. "They're going to kill us and no one will ever know what happened to us."

People were pounding on the roof and windows. If the hateful expressions on their faces were any indication, Sheila's prediction might prove to be accurate

"What could they want?" she shouted.

The only thing that came to mind was that we weren't who they thought we were. What could so many people in that part of the world have against two college kids from Idaho and Washington? With that in mind, I took our passports out of the glove compartment and held them up to the window.

When they saw the passports, people stopped shouting and pounding, put the car down and returned to the building from which they came. In less than a minute, the square was as deserted as it had been upon our arrival there.

"Let's get out of here," my bride said. "Step on it!"

No argument. We drove nonstop from there to the border with Greece, arriving in the wee hours. No one has ever been happier to pitch a tent in a field and collapse on rocky ground.

Until dawn—when we were awakened by a braying visitor poking its head through the flap of our tent. In the dark of the night, we unknowingly had pitched it in a field of donkeys.

No one has ever been able to explain why the crowd in Skopje seemed ready to tear us limb from limb. One explanation had to do with our Dutch license plates. Its source claimed that there was a feud between the Dutch and the Macedonians, but I haven't been able to verify that. If anyone reading this has a better explanation, I'd love to hear it.

Yugoslavia was intimidating, at times frightening. West Berlin was bright lights, modern buildings, streets filled with tourists and bustling Berliners. East Berlin was gray, grim, depressing.

To get there, we had to pass through a checkpoint where our car was carefully searched and driven over a mirror to check for contraband that could have been attached to the undercarriage. Stone-faced security police eyed us as suspiciously as if we were dangerous criminals. After passing their inspection and purchasing the required number of East German marks, worthless in the West, we were allowed to enter the city. The first person we encountered there was a young woman in tears.

"What's wrong?" I asked in my halting German.

She said she had just learned that her boyfriend had been fatally shot while trying to escape to the West by crossing the Gulf of Finland. It gave her hope to watch others be able to cross the Iron Curtain freely.

We happened to be there on the tenth anniversary of the completion of the Berlin Wall. Red and white banners promoting the anniversary were all that was colorful in the drab city. It was as if World War II had ended yesterday. Bombed buildings were yet to be cleared; streets were lined with rubble. Broad avenues were eerily deserted, the silence unnerving. We used our East German marks to buy a lunch of watery soup, bread, and terrible beer (could this really be Germany?), and gratefully returned to glittering West Berlin. When the wall came down eighteen years later, we rejoiced along with those freed at last. It was a victory not just for them, but for humanity.

We spent ten weeks in Europe, returning to Amsterdam in mid-August for the flight back to Seattle. My parents still hadn't arrived when we checked into the hotel. Nor were they on hand for the complimentary dinner that night, which was worrisome. It wasn't like them to be late, or to miss a free meal.

"Maybe they decided to stay at a hotel downtown," I said, pretending not to be worried. "We'll just meet them at the airport tomorrow."

They weren't at the airport, weren't on the plane home. Now we were really worried. Maybe *they'd* been killed by a mob.

The first thing I did upon landing in Seattle was call home.

Mom answered.

"Mom? What are you doing home? Why weren't you on the plane from Amsterdam?"

"We came home early," she said. "There was no way to get word to you. Daddy (she habitually called my father 'Daddy' rather than using his name) had a urinary infection."

"There weren't any urologists in Europe?"

"Well, you know how hard it is there with the language barrier and all."

Right. Who could forget the Germans beating around the bush with "guten tag"?

"Daddy wanted to come home early anyway. He wasn't having a very good time. I don't know why. I loved Europe."

Right. This was the woman who loved Europe so much she'd stormed out of a hotel to take the next plane home. Her take on their European vacation would live on in family lore for generations. Mom was nothing if not colorful.

Our summer as college students in Europe gave way to grownup responsibilities. Sheila's degree in speech therapy required her to spend a semester student teaching in Washington. She would stay with her parents in Olympia while I returned to Boise to look for a job and a place for us to live. With my degree from the Harvard of the West, the job part should be a cinch.

It wasn't. I applied at every daily newspaper in Idaho, from Boise and Pocatello in the southern part of the state to Saint Maries in the north. Not one of them was interested in snapping me up. The only one that granted me so much as an interview was *The Intermountain Observer*, in Boise. It was an excellent, firebrand weekly run by a first-rate journalist named Sam Day, who headed a staff of excellent reporters and columnists. Sam was polite, but not interested. He knew as well as anyone that good grades in college are no guarantee of journalistic excellence in the real world, and he had no shortage of applications from seasoned journalists.

Dad, who still dreamed of his son becoming a doctor or lawyer, suggested law school. I briefly considered it, but had no wish to return to the university for even a semester, let alone three years. I also considered chiropractic school. That would have pleased Dad. Not an MD, but still a doctor.

The immediate need, of course, was for a job. It may be common now for college graduates to live with their parents for months or years, but it was virtually unheard of then. A married, college-educated man sponging off his parents would have been an embarrassment. Spurned by virtually every newspaper in the state, I turned to the help-wanted ads.

The result was a job with National School Studios, a company that sent photographers to schools to take the pictures of elementary school students that would grace their parents' mantels and scrapbooks.

My boss was a long-suffering man named Hal. Long-suffering in the sense that he had taken so many school pictures for so long and trained so many assistants that he was bored with the job to the point of being jaded and bitter. He never said as much, but I suspected that he may have been even more long-suffering when it came to his marriage. His wife, who assisted with the business end of their partnership, was not a pleasant person. I think Hal was actually a pretty good guy at heart. Living with her could have made anyone bitter.

My week-long training consisted of accompanying him to schools in Boise to learn how to operate the camera and pose the students. My schedule for the second week, the first on my own, had me in schools outside of Boise but not too distant. This would soon change.

My salary was $150 a week, from which my travel expenses were deducted. As the travel demands increased, this became a problem. Paying for gas, meals, and motels was eating up so much of my income that in a town that was a six-hour drive from Boise I saved money by sleeping in my car one night. Hal was indignant upon learning this.

"You slept in your car? I can't have that! What if the people at the school had found out? We have an image to think about."

If the company was that concerned about its image, it should have paid employees' travel expenses. It was becoming clear why so many of Hal's assistants had been short-term.

One week when each of us was shooting schools in the same part of the state, he suggested that we meet for drinks after work. Over whiskey on the rocks, he confided that he hoped to retire before many more years and wondered whether I'd be interested in taking over his territory. I was too polite to say that if the job paid several times as much and the territory included a few thousand fewer square miles, I might consider it. As it was, I was driving hundreds of miles every week and working insane hours for practically nothing after deducting travel expenses.

The breaking point came the week I finished taking pictures at Howe Elementary School, in east-central Idaho, at four in the afternoon and had to be in Pendleton, Oregon, some 400 miles away, at eight the next morning. After deducting my travel expenses, I cleared ten bucks that week.

Hal didn't seem surprised when I quit. He'd watched the same scenario play out with God knows how many assistants.

"I guess that means you're not interested in taking over the territory someday," he said.

"Sorry, but no. It's just too much traveling."

"I could give you a raise."

"Hal, you could have given me a 50 percent raise and I would have only cleared $85 last week. With the number of hours I'm working, that isn't even minimum wage."

"All right," he reluctantly said. "Can you give me another week to find somebody else?"

"Okay, if you can keep the travel to under 200 or 300 miles that week."

He did. My last shoot was at a school an hour from Boise. Tearing down the equipment afterwards, I noticed that I'd forgotten to take the dark screen out of the camera before starting to take pictures that morning. The dark screen's purpose was always a bit of mystery to me, but the one thing I did know was that it had to be removed before taking pictures and reinserted when packing up after a day of shooting. If the dark screen wasn't taken out, no pictures could be taken. You could go through the motions, thinking you were taking pictures, but you weren't. I'd shot an entire school of several hundred students whose pictures didn't exist.

The proper thing to do would have been to tell Hal when returning the equipment, but it was his wife, not Hal, who greeted me at their door that night. He was there, but she was ready and waiting to get in a few final digs. I'd like to say I did the right thing and confessed, but her wrath would have been too much. It wasn't much of a stretch to imagine her clawing my eyes out, so I did the next best thing.

I said nothing.

I can only imagine their reaction upon realizing there were no pictures in the camera and that Hal would have to shoot the school over again. That it was my last assignment made it worse. Certain to think I did it on purpose to get even for the long hours and low pay, they'd have been justified in demanding that I reshoot the school on my own time. Or at the very least calling to say what they thought of me for pulling such a stunt.

I never heard a word from them.

In the greater scheme of things, it didn't matter. My last day with National School Studios was a Friday. That Saturday, *The Statesman*'s managing editor's secretary called. Would I be available for an interview?

So began the next forty years.

CHAPTER SEVEN
Welcome to The Daily Blab

The *Statesman's* managing editor's name was Dick Hronek. He asked me the standard questions about my background and, apparently satisfied with the answers, offered me a job as a reporter in the paper's Canyon County bureau.

The paper had bureaus in neighboring Canyon County, Twin Falls, and Ontario and Vale, Oregon. Today it has none.

"The job pays $115 a week," Hronek said.

A hundred and fifteen a week? I was being offered a job that would make use of my college education as a professional journalist and it would pay $35 a week *less* than I was making as an itinerant photographer?

On the other hand, there would be no travel expenses to deduct from my salary. No sleeping in my car, no weekly net incomes measured in double digits.

The offer was followed by a long pause. The salary ball was in my court.

"Would I have to live in Canyon County?"

"It would be best if you could live close to where you'd be working. But we could be flexible on that, at least for a while."

Another pause, a chance to mull it over. Turning the job down could have been career suicide. There had been no other offers from any of the other papers where I'd applied, and *The Statesman* not only was the state's largest paper but was conveniently located in my hometown. If I worked hard and proved myself, salary increases were sure to come.

"Okay. I accept."

"Great! Nice to have you aboard. My secretary will give you the paperwork we need to get you started."

Emerging from his office, elated to have a journalism job at last, I noticed a man who could have passed for Wild Bill Hickok's older brother staring intently at me from his spot at the copy desk. Seeing that the interview had ended, he accosted me on my way to meet the boss's secretary.

"You get the job?" he asked.

"Yes."

"How much they paying you?"

"A hundred and fifteen a week."

"Hmmm … Did he pause after telling you what the job paid?"

"Yeah! As a matter of fact, he did. A really long pause. How did you know that?"

"He does that with everybody. That was your chance to complain. If you had, you'd have gotten another ten bucks a week."

This was my introduction to Gordon Peterson, copy-desk chief, grammarian extraordinaire, and one of the newsroom's more colorful characters. He dressed like a cowboy. His graying blond hair spilled from his black cowboy hat to a few inches below his shoulders. His white beard reached the middle of his chest. His eyes were piercing blue, his face leathery, his fingers stained with nicotine.

In time, I would learn that every newspaper needs a Gordon Peterson. He was the gatekeeper, the person who more than anyone else kept grammatical, spelling and factual errors at bay. He had a discerning eye, encyclopedic knowledge of the language and the news, and a sardonic wit. He kept a bottle of whiskey in a drawer of his desk. That would be unheard of now and was frowned upon even then, but the editors knew his worth. He was allowed a few small rebellions.

We were lamenting the loss of my additional ten bucks a week when the police radio, monitored 24/7, bought word of a car crash with injuries.

"Want to do a story while you're waiting for the paperwork?" Peterson asked.

"A story? Me?"

"Sure. You're a reporter, aren't you? Call the cops and give us a few paragraphs on that car crash. You can use that empty desk over there."

This was unexpected. My training to date hadn't included calling cops or writing stories about accidents. More than a little nervous, I looked up the number for the police department and haltingly asked for whoever knew something about car crashes.

"You're new, aren't you?" the voice on the other end of the line said.

"How did you know?"

"You didn't ask for dispatch. I'll connect you."

The dispatcher provided the basic details—where and how the accident happened, vehicles involved, victims transported to a local hospital. I took notes and wrote a brief story, agonizing over every word. When it was finished, I handed it to Peterson.

"It doesn't go to me first," he said. "I'm the slot man. It goes to me last."

The slot man was the person who sat in the center of a large, horseshoe-shaped copy desk. The people who sat on the desk's edges were collectively known as rim men. The rim men got the stories when the city editor or state editor finished editing them. They in turn edited them and gave them to the slot man for the final editing. Because I hadn't been assigned an editor yet and the accident story was hardly stop-the-presses material, I was told not to bother the city editor and give my story to one of the rim men. All but one of the copy desk editors were, in fact, men. Copy editors worked night shifts, which allowed time for reporters and editors who worked days to write and edit the stories that would go to the copy desk. Copy editors worked until deadline, usually around midnight.

"Good story," one of the rim men said after reading what I'd written and handing it over to Peterson.

Kind words remembered for life. It was a nothing story, three, maybe four paragraphs of forgettable details about a routine accident. But it was my very first newspaper story, and the rim man's kindness meant a lot. Almost as much as seeing it in print the next morning and sailing on Cloud Nine to the breakfast table at my parents' house.

"Did you read the story about the car crash?" I asked them.

"Car crash?" Mom asked.

"What car crash?" Dad asked.

"The one in the paper. Didn't you read it? It's on the second page of the local news section."

"Hmmm. No, we missed that one."

"You should read it then. It's a good story."

They read it.

"What's so special about it? Seems pretty routine."

"I wrote it. That's what's special about it. It's my first story!"

"You wrote this?"

"Yes."

"We thought you hadn't actually started yet."

"Well, no. I haven't. But as long as I was there yesterday, they asked me to cover that car crash."

"Did they now? Good for you! It is a well-written story, actually. A little short, but nicely written and it tells you pretty much everything you need to know about the accident."

I clipped and saved that little story for a while, but eventually it was lost or thrown away. There was nothing special about it other than its being my first words in print, and other stories would follow.

The Statesman building could not have been more conveniently located for reporters. It was downtown, catty corner from City Hall, a block from the Statehouse, and within walking distance of numerous government offices, corporate headquarters, and other businesses. The paper's owners had tried for years to purchase a home immediately east of it for a needed expansion, but the home's owner refused to sell. He hated *The Statesman* and spurned ever increasing offers, declaring that the paper would get it over his dead body. He died a month after the Gannett Co., which purchased the paper just before I started working there, committed to buying a site for a new building inconveniently located miles from downtown. His heirs would have sold it in a heartbeat.

The old newsroom was something out of another time. Computers were still a few years away. Hot lead no longer was being used, but the Linotype machines that previously were used to set it were still in the building.

Compared with the way newspapers operate today, with journalists often working from home on laptops and their stories being sent to press with a few key strokes, the process used then seems almost primitive. Reporters wrote their stories on typewriters, many of them decades old. The paper used wasn't typing paper. It was off-white with a grainy texture. Every desk was equipped with a glue gun. Glue guns resembled old-fashioned oil cans. When reporters finished their stories, they glued the ends of the pages together to create a ribbon of paper that, depending on the length of the story, could be anywhere from a couple of feet to several yards in length. Stories were double-spaced to allow room for editing marks, made with soft-lead pencils.

Reporters carried their finished stories to their respective editors, who either edited them and sent them on to the copy desk or returned them to the reporters for additional work. When an editor was satisfied with a story, he shouted "copy," summoning a copy boy who would carry it to the copy desk and place it in a wire basket. A rim man would retrieve it from the basket, check the spelling, grammar, and factual accuracy and send it to the slot man, Peterson, for its final editing. A story that for whatever reason—incomplete, libelous, in poor taste, etc.—was deemed unworthy of making the paper was "spiked." The copy desk had a sharp spike on a metal base, upon which doomed stories were impaled—the worst thing that could happen to one of your stories. "Spiked" was synonymous with "failure." It was a good piece of jargon, though. The word "spiked" was strong, unambiguous, dreaded. Alas, it has vanished from journalism's lexicon. If you said it to a young journalist now, he or she would look at you as blankly as if you'd said a good story was the bee's knees.

Copy desk editors, Peterson excepted, looked almost as if they were wearing uniforms—cheap slacks, white shirts, and narrow ties, usually black. Some wore eyeshades to cut the glare from the overhead fluorescent lights. Peterson occasionally wore an eyeshade, but that's where any resemblance to the other copy editors' accoutrements ended. He wouldn't have been caught dead wearing a white shirt or a tie. He wore cowboy shirts with designs embroidered on them. He actually had been a cowboy once and had previously worked at *The Tombstone Epitaph*, famous for its coverage of Wyatt Earp, Doc Holiday and the Gunfight at the OK Corral. He unfailingly wore cowboy hats, cowboy boots, a bandana, and occasionally chaps to work.

My first afternoon at *The Statesman* had been a success. I'd been hired as a working journalist, written a story that appeared in print, and been introduced to the newsroom and some of its denizens. But my first official day wouldn't be until the following Monday. That's when the real work, the actual test of my abilities, would begin.

When I arrived for work that morning, a giant of man beckoned to me from the elevator that went from the first-floor lobby to the second-floor newsroom.

"Hey, Woodward!" he yelled. "Get in and we'll ride up together."

The outsized character was Jim Poore, a sports writer and another unforgettable individual. Jim stood several inches over six feet and tipped the scales at well over 300 pounds. He knew my name because we'd attended Boise High School together. Though his class was one ahead of mine and he was enormously popular while I was a faceless Saint Teresa's transfer, he'd remembered my name.

"I hear you're the new guy in the Canyon County Bureau," he said as we rode the elevator together.

"That's right."

"Well, hopefully you won't be there long. If you do a good job there and a beat opens up in Boise you could probably get it. Have you met Miriam Barr yet?"

"No. Who's Miriam Barr?"

"You'll be working with her in the Canyon County Bureau. She's a character."

It was becoming apparent that *The Statesman* was something of a magnet for characters.

"Have you met your editor yet?" Poore asked.

"No. They told me his name was Steve something."

"Steve Ahrens, the state editor. Seems like an okay guy."

The state editor was in charge of the reporters who worked in the hinterland of the bureaus. Those who worked out of the main office in Boise reported to the city editor.

Poore was right about Ahrens. He was an okay guy—welcoming, friendly, eager to show his new charge the ropes.

The first story I wrote for him never saw print. My assignment for the day was to cover the Idaho Sheepmen's Convention. The sheep industry was a big deal in Idaho, then still a largely agricultural state, and its annual convention warranted a sizable story. I was to attend the convention, which was being held in the nicest hotel in town, and write a story about it. My story, however, would be only a learning tool. The real story, the one the paper would publish, would be written by Bob Lorimer, a longtime agricultural reporter and popular columnist. I had grown up hearing my folks cite his beloved "Boiseana" column. They never dreamed that their son would meet him, let alone become one of his colleagues.

At the convention, I furiously scribbled sheep notes. It was far from being the last time I'd wish that my high school education had included shorthand as well as typing. Why the journalism school at the University of Idaho didn't include shorthand as a requirement for future reporters was beyond me. It would easily have been one of the most useful skills we could have acquired. I repeatedly fell behind in my notes on what the convention's speakers were saying and returned to the newsroom in a near panic. Handing over a desperately cobbled story based on woefully incomplete notes could, I feared, be my first and last official act as a

Statesman employee.

Ahrens, however, couldn't have been nicer about it. He used the story for the learning tool it was, patiently explaining what was right and wrong with it. Afraid to leave out something that might be important (what did a city kid like me know about raising sheep?), I had included everything—even the governor's jokes. Ahrens compared my story with Lorimer's, explaining how he had zeroed in on the most newsworthy aspects and left out what was unimportant. I learned more about real-world, deadline reporting that day than I did in two years of college journalism.

Though Hronek hadn't insisted that I live in Canyon County, he made it clear that I would need to live closer to Canyon County than Boise. Sheila had just finished her student teaching in Olympia, and we found an apartment we could afford in Meridian, then a largely agricultural community of 2,600 souls reasonably close to the Canyon County line. (Meridian today is Idaho's second-largest city, with a population of 115,000.) Our small apartment had stark white walls and cheap shag carpet. The gap between the floor and the bottom of the front door was big enough to roll a golf ball through with room left over. It was cheerless, hard to heat, utterly lacking in character. Happily, we wouldn't be there long.

The Caldwell bureau was a twenty-minute drive away. Occupying half of a small building on a downtown corner, it was just big enough for two desks, a couple of filing cabinets, and a Teletype machine. Teletypes were bulky, clattering devices that printed breaking wire (Associated Press and United Press International) stories. Ours could also be used to receive and respond to messages from the Boise newsroom. A woman of indeterminate age, with dark eyes and a tanned face that contrasted strikingly with her snow white hair was waiting for us. This was the redoubtable Miriam Barr, the character Poore had mentioned on the elevator. Ahrens, who had accompanied me to the bureau office, introduced us, left with a few parting words and headed back to the Mother Ship. I envied him. Compared with the pulsing Boise newsroom with its urgency and abundance of interesting people, the quiet bureau office seemed like a tomb.

Miriam wasted no time instructing me on what was hers and what was mine. A desk and typewriter were mine. The other desk and the file cabinets were hers, as was the gleaming black Underwood typewriter on her desk. Practically an antique, it was in mint condition. Under no circumstance, she admonished me, was I to touch her typewriter.

Her beat included the local courts, the Nampa City Council and school board, and the sheriff's department. My beat was pretty much everything else: the Caldwell City Council, school board, and police department and, time permitting, an occasional feature story. I was more than welcome to write the features. Miriam had little use for them. She almost never did any, and then reluctantly.

Feature stories and photography quickly became my meat and potatoes. I did the hard news stories out of a sense of duty and because they had to be done, but I found local government meetings monotonous. Born reporters enjoy government reporting, live to do hard news stories, and are very good at it. I turned out to be more of a shirttail journalist, a second cousin to the real thing. I was always happiest when the reporting was done and I could sit down and put the words together. If I couldn't be the next Steinbeck, perhaps I could make a name for myself as a journalist with a flair for writing interesting features. And maybe, at some point in the future, opinion pieces.

The feature stories came quickly and easily. I wrote one whenever a likely subject presented itself. The editors must have liked them because before long they started appearing at the bottom of the front page, often with a cartoon drawn by John Collias. Collias was a local artist who freelanced occasional story illustrations in addition to doing a pen-and-ink drawing for a Sunday op-ed page feature, "Portrait of a Distinguished Citizen." One of my feature stories, a satire on the failure of that year's legislative session to accomplish much of substance, won the state press club's award for editorial writing. Gratifying as it was to win, it was an insult to veteran editorial writers who day in and day out addressed important issues. I was as embarrassed as I was flattered to receive it.

My photos occasionally made the paper, though rarely on the front page. I used the Pentax camera purchased while in the Navy to take pictures of whatever struck me as being visually interesting, often timeless pictures that weren't tied to stories and could run whenever a filler photo was needed.

One day a Teleype message from Ahrens asked the bureau people to be on the lookout for weather art. It was winter and just beginning to snow so off I went. My search was rewarded at a golf course where two elderly gentlemen were putting on a snowy green, both dressed as Scotsmen—kilts, tam-'o-shanters, the works. Quarter-sized snowflakes fell heavily around them—perfect weather art. I took lots of pictures and sent the film to Ahrens, confidently expecting one of them to be the next day's weather picture.

It wasn't. No golfers, no snowstorm. Hoping the picture was being held, I looked for it again the next day and the day after that. Nothing.

The following week, an envelope arrived in the mail. Inside were my negatives and a note saying, "Tim, these are nice pictures of these golfers, but there are black spots all over the negatives."

The spots, of course, were the snowflakes. I've occasionally teased Ahrens about it over the years. Good naturedly, of course.

It soon became apparent that driving to and from Meridian every day wasn't practical. It took valuable time, and the Fiat on slick roads might as well have been a toboggan. We found a nicer apartment for less money in Caldwell. Signing a six-month lease was required so we made sure to ask what would happen to our damage deposit if *The Statesman* transferred me to Boise before the six months were up.

"That wouldn't be a problem," the landlord said. "If it's a work-related transfer we wouldn't hold you to it."

He and his wife seemed like honest people. They were forever quoting scripture. We signed the lease.

Five and half months later, *The Statesman* transferred me to Boise.

"We'll get our damage deposit back, right?" (There was no damage, and we left the apartment cleaner than we'd found it.)

"No. I'm sorry, but it hasn't been six months."

"But you said it wouldn't be a problem if I was transferred. And it's only two weeks short of six months."

"Sorry."

It was my first but not last unpleasant experience with people who wear their religion on their shirtsleeves but don't practice it.

My successor in the Caldwell bureau was a young man named Bill Hathaway. He hadn't been there long when he made the mistake of using Miriam's typewriter. She was out of the office at the time, and Hathaway couldn't resist its gleaming beauty and soft touch. He was partway through his story when, to his surprise, Miriam came to work early and caught him in the act.

"What did she do?" I asked him.

"You won't believe it," he replied. "She picked it up and threw it across the office."

My front-page feature stories impressed the bosses enough for them to promote me to the Mother Ship, but not in the way I'd hoped for or envisioned. The job that opened up there would get me back home to Boise, but it had nothing to do with feature writing.

I was to be *The Statesman*'s new city-county government reporter

CHAPTER EIGHT
Reporter

My new beat included Boise's city council and planning and zoning commission, its urban renewal agency, the county commission and highway district, and a newly formed council of governments. Almost all of them, especially for a new reporter with limited government reporting experience, would prove to be powder kegs.

My first assignment was to interview a Chinese gentleman who was being evicted from his longtime home at the epicenter of the city's urban renewal project. Boise had once had a thriving Chinatown, but by then it was all but gone. He was its last resident. His name was Billy Fong.

"Billy Fong is moving out today," my new editor, Jim Golden, told me. "He's leaving to live with relatives in San Francisco. You need to go to his apartment and interview him. This will probably be a front-page story. He could be leaving any time so you need to get right over there."

Golden was not a man to be crossed. He was known to have thrown his telephone and even his chair across the newsroom in fits of consuming rage. I got right over there.

Billy Fong was big news. The newspaper and the local television stations all had done numerous stories about the Boise Redevelopment Agency's long-running efforts to evict him. When I arrived at Fong's home, he was nowhere to be seen. The apartment building where he lived already was being demolished. One wall of the apartment where he had lived was gone.

"Have you seen Billy Fong?" I asked one of the workmen.

"The old guy who lived here?"

"Right."

"He left this morning. I heard he went to San Francisco."

My first big assignment, a potential front-page story, and I was too late. Desperate to salvage something—anything—I poked around in what was left of Billy's apartment, took some notes, and trudged back to the paper to write my story.

The story duly reported that the last resident of the urban renewal district had departed to live with relatives in San Francisco and went on to describe the place where he had lived. The description included a line that would haunt me for months:

"If a three-foot pile of empty tuna fish cans on the living room floor is an indication, the cleaning lady hadn't been in lately."

My phone was ringing when I reported for work the next morning.

"Are you the person who wrote that vile story on Page One this morning?"

This was not the reaction I'd hoped for with my first big story on my new beat.

Told that I was the person who had written the vile story, the caller berated me in withering terms for violating a person's privacy and making a snide remark about his housekeeping, or lack of it, on the front page of the newspaper. I later learned that the caller was the wife of Gordon Peterson, our esteemed copy desk chief. How my lapse of judgment got past him was a mystery. Maybe it was his night off.

More angry calls followed, as did a barrage of angry letters to the editor. The letters continued for weeks, likening me to everyone from Hitler to Charles Manson. One opined that I must not even be capable of loving my wife.

One of the few offended people who didn't write a scathing letter was Billy Fong himself. If you're still alive and happen to read this, Billy, I am truly sorry. I was young, desperate for a story, and had volumes to learn about the power of hurtful words in print.

My second assignment was a story on the county highway district adopting its annual budget. Shown to the budget director's office, I introduced myself as the new *Statesman* reporter and told him I was there to do a report on the budget. His reaction was the only memorable thing about an otherwise ho-hum assignment.

"You're the new *Statesman* reporter?"

"That's right."

"I wouldn't use *The Statesman* to start a fire in my fireplace."

Dislike of the newspaper was hardly uncommon. Idaho was and is an ultraconservative state, where complaints about "that liberal *Statesman*" are regularly voiced. This has always struck me as odd because in many ways *The Statesman* has a history of being quite conservative. It has, through the years, endorsed numerous conservative Republican candidates, and supported conservative positions. Supporting even one liberal or progressive position, however, is one too many for some readers. And it only takes one story deemed to be of the wrong political bent, in poor taste or containing an egregious error to turn a reader against a newspaper, sometimes for life.

The highway district and its budget were relatively low priorities. The big story in Boise in the early 1970s, the one everyone was talking about and that occasionally made national headlines, was the urban renewal project.

Urban renewal was a federally subsidized program to reduce urban blight in inner cities. Blighted areas were taken by eminent domain, leveled, and rebuilt by private developers. A worthy goal, perhaps, in larger cities that actually had urban blight. Boise didn't have an inner city or a blighted area, at least not in comparison with those in many big cities. Nevertheless, the renewal project was approved for federal funding, dominated the local news, and would quite literally tear the city apart.

The renewal area was the downtown business district. Boise actually had had a rather nice downtown prior to urban renewal: four theaters, five department stores, shops, banks, hotels, corporate headquarters, some excellent restaurants, and some colorful bars and taverns. With the coming of urban renewal, many were destined for the wrecking ball.

The result was years of demolition, frustration, failure. One storied building after another was razed. Entire blocks of what had once been viable businesses were reduced to rubble and weedy parking lots. A Chicago newspaper referred to Boise as "the city that tried to tear itself down."

Visitors to downtown Boise could be forgiven for thinking it had been bombed. Block after block was partially or wholly leveled. Those where the wrecking ball had razed all of the structures were converted to parking lots, largely unused because many of the things that had attracted people to downtown were gone. Mountains of rubble and crumbling wall remnants reminiscent of postwar London or Berlin comprised the blocks still being razed.

Public criticism was intense, as was competition to cover the story. My primary adversary on the beat was a woman who worked for what was then the dominant local news station. A generation older than I was, Paulie Crooke was smart, tough, fiercely competitive. She also had the advantage of working for a news director who was a city council member, their bosses seemingly failing to recognize a conflict of interest. We worked like demons to scoop each other.

Paulie went on to become the station's news director, the first female news director in the country, and work for CBS Network News. To honor her as the first female television news director, CBS invited her to an awards luncheon in New York City. Years later, over lunch, she told me she learned at the last minute that she was to follow Walter Cronkite at the podium. She also confessed over lunch that day—we'd become friends rather than adversaries by then—that she had cried after I scooped her on a big story.

She got me back on a bigger story the very next week. Competition like that has largely become a memory. After retiring, I called *The Statesman* a number of times with tips on stories only to see one of the television stations do them first. When the death of rock star Paul Revere was imminent, I told an editor so the paper could have a story ready. Paul's wife, Sydney Revere, gave me private numbers for his band members, longtime agent, Nancy Sinatra, and Righteous Brother Bill Medley to pass on to *The Statesman* for quotes from them when the time came.

It came on a Saturday evening. Sydney called to tell me, and I tried to tell *The Statesman*. I called every newsroom extension I could think of, got no one and left multiple messages. No story appeared in the next day's paper. The reporter assigned to have the story ready to go when Paul died had done virtually nothing. It fell to a rookie reporter working the Sunday shift to scramble together a story, which contained enough errors that a front-page correction had to be published the following day. Despite having a week's head start, *The Statesman* was scooped by other newspapers, the local television stations, even network news. So much for giving my old paper a heads-up.

The turning point for Boise trying to tear itself down was opposition to tearing down the Egyptian Theater. Downtown's other beautiful and historic old theater, the Pinney, had already been demolished to put up a parking lot that exists to this day. The Egyptian, with its frescoed pillars, winged scarab and other Egyptian-style carvings, was destined for a similar fate. With the wrecking ball looming, only a public outcry and the intervention of public-spirited citizens saved it. Today, the beloved landmark is a popular concert venue and gathering place.

The urban renewal goal, the dream that bedeviled successive city and redevelopment agency administrations, was to build a downtown shopping mall. Though malls are common as weeds today, a mall was something Boise lacked at the time. Smaller

Idaho cities had malls, but the capital and largest city did not. The redevelopers' theory was that building a regional shopping mall in a central, downtown location would bring needed department stores and shops in addition to facilitating orderly growth and discouraging urban sprawl.

Artists' renderings of the mall, however, resembled nothing so much as a collection of giant Quonset huts. That people would flock to such a place seemed unlikely except in the minds of the planners and officials who were promoting it. Add to that the difficulties of providing access to what would have been the state's largest shopping mall in the center of its downtown business district, and in hindsight it's hard to believe that anyone seriously believed it could happen.

Successive developers were hired and quit or were fired. Department store chains were feverishly courted. High hopes alternated with crushing disappointments. Department store chains waffled, never saying no outright but never quite committing. The atmosphere at the redevelopment agency meetings I covered varied from hopeful to funereal.

The agency's executive director was the most nervous man I've ever known. His name was Gary Hughes. He stammered and fidgeted continually during agency board meetings. More than once he called me at home to ask what I'd written in my coverage of the meetings and plead with me to omit or soft-pedal negative developments before the stories could go to press. It was painful to tell him I couldn't do that. I liked Gary and felt sorry for him. The job clearly was killing him.

Literally. They found him in his back yard, where he'd fatally shot himself.

The mall's death knell came in an announcement by the J. C. Penny Co. that it had quit waffling and would not build a downtown store. It had been obvious for some time that department store chains preferred the suburbs, but that hadn't stopped city officials from doggedly pursuing the doomed downtown mall idea. In a statement that was equal parts naivety and sour grapes, Boise's then-mayor accused Penny's of "leading us down the primrose lane."

Having had their fill of rubble and futility, the voters elected a new city administration that abandoned the downtown mall plan in favor of building a mall in the suburbs and a public square, the Grove, where the downtown mall would have been. The result was a new Boise.

The suburban mall, Boise Towne Square, was instantly popular and remains one of Idaho's largest and most successful shopping malls more than thirty years after it was completed. The Grove remains the heart of a vibrant, present-day downtown. Ringed by a convention center, a multipurpose arena, banks, shops, and restaurants, it's a popular venue for everything from concerts to ice hockey to kids playing in its courtyard fountain.

Construction of Boise Towne Square ended decades of pent up demand—Boiseans at last had their shopping mall—and launched a period of extraordinary growth. In 1972, the year I started on the urban renewal beat, Boise's population was approximately 75,000. Downtown had two "high-rise" buildings, both with fewer than twenty stories. Traffic was minimal. You could drive from one end of the city to another in about ten minutes. The city was growing, but it still felt in some ways like a small town. When you went to a store, a movie, a restaurant, or other business, you expected to see people you knew. Much of the land between Boise and Meridian was still farmland.

With the completion of Boise Town Square, that began to change, and change rapidly. As of this writing, Boise's population is three times what it was in 1972. Its downtown has been made over with so many tall buildings and new businesses that I've gotten lost there. Lost, in the city where I grew up and have spent most of my life. Gridlock is a daily fact of life. Instead of ten minutes, it can take an hour or more to drive across town. So many newcomers live in the city now that it's unusual to see a familiar face in a crowd, and most of the farmland between Boise, Meridian, and Nampa has been developed.

I often think of my father, who died in 1985 and was keen on any aspect of growth. He used to say that "someday there'll be a quarter of a million people in this valley." Now there are three times that many. Dad wouldn't recognize Boise today.

To prepare for the growth they knew was coming, local officials formed a a council consisting of a county commissioner and the mayors of Boise and the four smaller cities in Ada County. They hired a staff of professional planners with a goal of making Boise a model city. Boise, they said, was still small enough that with smart planning it could avoid the problems of growth that many other cities had experienced.

The Ada Council of Governments (ACOG) was a worthy experiment that ended in failure. Urban planners recruited from around the country comprised its staff. Their director was a man named Robert McAbee, a planning administrator who also had been an executive with the World Council of Churches. I came to know and admire him during my time on the local government beat. He was a highly principled man who was devoted to the cause of making Boise an example of what good planning could accomplish.

The most controversial thing to emerge from the work he oversaw was what became known as the urban containment plan. It essentially meant drawing a boundary around Boise and not allowing development to occur outside of it.

For developers, this was anathema. The plan was reviled as everything from overreach to Communism. The development forces rose up against not just the plan but against the council of governments itself. They recruited a right-leaning television repairman to run for the county commission and its swing vote on the ACOG board. His first official move upon being elected was to call for a vote to disband the council of governments. The vote passed, the council was disbanded, and the hope of making Boise a model city went with it.

I was then several years from becoming a regular columnist, but I wrote an editorial page column pointing out the preponderance of development interests on local councils and commissions. The mayor's immediate predecessor was a developer. A majority of seats on its city council and planning and zoning commissions were held by developers or real estate agents. The proverbial foxes guarding the henhouse.

Reaction to the column was outrage rivaling that of the Billy Fong Affair. Woodward the Terrible again dominated the Letters to the Editor. At an appointment to interview them for a story, not one of the three county commissioners would say a single word to me. The real estate agents rose up en masse, demanding that I be fired and pulling their advertising from the newspaper until it happened. In those days, that was a sizable chunk of advertising. Real estate ads often comprised several pages of the paper. Losing them would cost *The Statesman* thousands.

The publisher at the time was Robert B. Miller Jr. A native of Battle Creek, Michigan, Miller became the publisher when the Gannett Corp., bought Federated Publications, which included *The Statesman* and half a dozen other newspapers. Miller's father was the head of Federated, so Bob had some clout.

To his credit, he stuck with me. He told the realtors they had no business dictating editorial policy or who was hired or fired at the newspaper. The realtors kept their ads out of the paper for about two weeks, the time it took for them to realize they were hurting themselves more than me.

A few years later, we received a letter saying that the term "Realtor" had been trademarked and demanding that in future stories we print the entire word in upper case letters, followed by the trademark symbol, which would have looked ridiculous. The editors met the realtors partway, using an upper case "R," but stopping short of using all capitals or the trademark symbol. I continued to use a lower case "R," even knowing that the copy editors would change it. A futile gesture, but the memory of the realtors trying to get me fired still rankled. It also seemed more accurate. I'd known some pretty lower case realtors.

I'd been working for the paper for six months when we moved to *The Statesman's* new building on Curtis Road, the country lane I'd known as a child. Growth had transformed it into a four-lane arterial street lined by a regional medical center, doctors' offices, schools, a hotel, and other businesses. The new building was modern and functional, but with none of the charm of the old one downtown.

The public was invited to an open house when it opened. My folks attended and were favorably impressed. Dad was especially impressed upon meeting Bob Miller, who was always impeccably and tastefully dressed.

"You might want to consider him as a role model," Dad said, taking me aside. "If you work hard and apply yourself, you might have his job someday."

Dad never gave up. I'd never be a doctor or a lawyer, but a newspaper publisher might be an acceptable substitute.

We'd barely moved into the new building when we had our first casualty. Jerry Schifferdecker, the courts reporter, disappeared one night on deadline. He should have been at his desk, putting the finishing touches on a story. One of the copy editors went looking for him and found him on the floor in the men's room, where he'd suffered a fatal heart attack. Not a good omen for our new digs.

Nor was an assault, not long afterwards. Our education reporter came home from work one evening and was stabbed by an intruder in her home. The wound wasn't life threatening, but it was serious enough that she was hospitalized. Police investigated, but the assailant never was apprehended, the motive never known. Whether the attack was related to her reporting, her personal life, or was completely random remained a mystery.

My desk in the new newsroom was next to that of Bob Lorimer, the agricultural reporter and popular columnist. Decades later, I remember some of his opening lines:

"I woke up yesterday to the sound of snow falling.

"Oh, yes you can!"

That column went on to describe the "sound," actually a feeling, that accompanies the absence of sound caused by falling snow.

"My wife is scraping the house so she can paint it again, even though she knows it disturbs my naps. I told her to convince herself that the color it already is is her favorite color."

A Jehovah's Witness, he complained every December when the newsroom Christmas tree arrived.

"Here comes the Hanukkah bush again."

If you watched closely, though, you could see a twinkle in his eye.

Betty Penson was the redoubtable editor of what was still known as the society section. Her byline was a drawing of a bee, a pen, and a sun, for B. Penson. She had traveled the world on complimentary airline junkets to write about everything from her exploits in European capitals to dining with Ethiopian Emperor Haile Selassie. She had been at the paper forever and, as I would learn, she was not a woman to be crossed.

I realized this somewhat painfully after writing a humor column comparing her story about staying in a luxury hotel and dining at gourmet restaurants in Victoria, British Columbia, with mine of having so little money as a college student there that I spent a night sleeping on the floor of a house under construction. Penson responded with a blistering column about the upstart who she thought was poking fun at her. My name continued to appear condescendingly in her columns from time to time from then until her retirement.

John Corlett was known as "the dean of Idaho political columnists." A dapper man never seen without a tie and jacket, he had covered numerous legislative sessions and national political conventions, interviewed governors, senators, and presidents. Belying his formidable reputation, he was also the nicest of men—unassuming, modest, willing to help even the greenest rookie.

Wilder Bellamy spent only a few months as a reporter, but made a lasting impression. He threw a "Welcome, Wilder" party in his apartment after a week or two on the job, spending an impressive amount of money on alcoholic beverages, mixers, and hors d'oeuvres. He was the general assignment reporter the night a fire broke out in a downtown building. Peterson and other editors huddled around the copy desk awaiting word on whether the fire was serious enough to remake the front page. Wilder's voice crackled through a phone speaker.

"I'm approaching the scene of the fire."

Moments later, "I'm at the scene of the fire."

Then, "I've passed the scene of the fire."

The copy desk erupted with shouts.

"Wilder, turn around! Wilder, go back!"

Wilder was a sweet guy; he just wasn't cut out to be a reporter. I often wonder what became of him. His name alone—Wilder Bellamy—made for one of the more memorable bylines ever to appear in *The Statesman*. It would have been perfect for a 1940s movie star.

Jim Poore, who had accosted me in the elevator on my first day and had recently been promoted to sports editor, was larger than life, literally and figuratively. He tipped the scales at 325 pounds and despite good intentions to lose weight was powerless to resist food cravings.

"Hey, Woodward," he would say, usually when I was on deadline. "Let's go down to the Fanci-Freeze and get a Boston Shake," a specialty of the house, consisting of a chocolate milk shake poured over a hot fudge sundae.

A fellow sportswriter accompanying him on a trip to Sun Valley waited patiently while Poore ordered a family-sized combination pizza and a pitcher of Coke.

"That will be right out," the waitress said as she walked away.

"Wait!" Poore's dinner companion shouted after her. "I'd like something to eat, too."

His charm was as outsized as his appetite. Poore could talk almost anybody into almost anything, as I learned the day he broached his plan to have the paper send us to the Soviet Union to write about what life was like behind the Iron Curtain. This at a time when even an overnight trip to another Idaho city had to be approved in advance by the executive editor.

The executive editor listened to Poore's Soviet Union pitch and to my astonishment gave us the green light. I was astonished again when a customs officer in Moscow's Sheremetyevo airport discovered "contraband," two *Playboy* magazines, in Jim's luggage. We had been warned that such magazines were considered pornographic and were banned in the USSR, and that possessing them could land their owners in prison. Jim thought that was a capital idea.

"Just think of what a great story we'd have if they sent us to the Gulag," he said.

The customs officer let us off with a stern warning, confiscated the magazines and sent us on our way. Jim was genuinely disappointed.

Two years later, enamored of a book about haunted places in Britain, he proposed the two of us going there to check them out.

"Fine, Jim. I'll go with you while you pitch it, but I'm not saying a word. When the boss laughs us out of his office, it will be your fault, not mine."

We spent the next two weeks in Britain, chasing ghosts. We never found any, but we did get the chills a few times in some truly creepy places.

Jim's junkets were a welcome relief from the routine of covering the city council, county commission, and various other boards, agencies, committees, etc. I spent three years on the local government beat, which was more than enough. By my third round of annexation hearings, I knew what people whose homes would be annexed would say before they said it. My hero by then had become one of my predecessors on the beat. Legend had it that during a city council meeting he reacted to a council member's inane comment by standing up, throwing his notebook in the air, and shouting, "That's the stupidest thing I've ever heard." He was fired, but his name was spoken with reverence by the reporters who followed him.

It must have been apparent to the bosses that I'd reached the burnout point with the local government beat. I was wondering how many more meetings I could stand to cover when they made me an investigative reporter for a summer. I would be working with the permanent investigative reporter, Ken Matthews.

Matthews was good at investigating, but not good at connecting the dots in his writing. He spent months working on his stories. They typically filled two full pages of the newspaper. The problem was that after wading through his prose, readers were left with the impression that somebody had done something wrong but weren't quite sure who or what it was. The bosses wanted me to work with him to try to make sense of his stories.

Matthews quickly lost interest in our first collaboration. He was preoccupied with what he was sure was a bigger story, leaving me to finish it on my own. It had to do with the Highway Beautification Act, unofficially known as the "Lady Bird Act" because it was the pet project of Lady Bird Johnson, the wife of ex-President Lyndon Johnson. Its goal was to beautify the nation's highways by providing states with money to purchase unsightly billboards and tear them down. Matthews had suspected something amiss in the way the act was being administered in Idaho, and his hunch proved to be right. I spent a good part of the summer investigating a company that owned many of the signs and was being paid what appeared to be exorbitant amounts of money for them. Further investigation found that the company was owned by none other than the state administrator of the program, who was anonymously buying the signs cheap and selling them to the state for a fat profit. My stories led to a state investigation and his subsequent imprisonment.

That done, I was assigned to help Matthews with his "big story." He'd been working on it for months, had finished the reporting and needed help writing it. His first draft was true to form. A serious white-collar crime had been committed, but what and by whom wasn't clear. We spent a couple of weeks working together to make it comprehensible. The story ran on the front page of the Sunday paper with a "jump" to multiple inside pages. Reading it over breakfast, I choked on my pancakes. Unable to leave the story alone once it had been put to bed, Matthews had returned to the paper the night before and done some last-minute tinkering just before deadline. The result was a grave factual error necessitating a front-page retraction written by *The Statesman's* lawyers.

Another retraction followed not long afterwards, this one in a special section that someone had sabotaged by inserting embarrassing typos.

The Statesman had had a long tradition of embarrassing typos and maladroit headlines. A headline on Miss America being crowned appeared next to one saying "Nixon Asks For Peace." A story about the Boise State University football team's backfield, dubbed "the Four Horsemen," referred to them as "the Four Hosemen." Matthews, who was something of a malcontent, was suspected of being the culprit responsible.

My collaboration with him coincided with summer's end, and a new assignment was waiting. Various editors had by this point spent almost four years trying to break my habit of editorializing, subtly or not so subtly sneaking my opinions into my news stories. Their diligence paid off. I stopped, or mostly stopped, editorializing. By the time I was consistently resisting the temptation to work in an opinion that the editors were sure to cut, they gave up and made me an editorial writer.

My new boss, the editorial page editor, was Ken Robison, a thoughtful, studious man who had won national awards for editorial writing. I had once overheard him talking to my previous boss—shouting, actually—about one of my news stories: "I don't care what he thinks about it! What he thinks shouldn't be in his story."

When I had amassed a total of not quite two weeks on the editorial-writing job, Robison surprised me with some disconcerting news.

"I'm leaving on vacation next week," he said. "I'm going backpacking in the primitive area (now the Frank Church River of No Return Wilderness). You'll be in charge of the editorial page. I'll be gone for four weeks."

"Four weeks? I have to come up with all of the subjects, write all the editorials, and lay out the pages for four weeks? I don't even know how to lay out pages."

"Don't worry," he replied. "The editorial board will decide the subjects, and the copy desk people can help with the layouts. You'll be fine."

The editorial board was made up of the publisher, the top editors, and the editorial writers. It decided the issues that would be addressed and the positions the newspaper would take on them. Usually this was done with a majority vote.

In one memorable instance, I was the only person on the board who was against capital punishment and was assigned to write an editorial supporting it. The next day, a reader called to say it was "the most left-handed endorsement of capital punishment I've ever read." Sneaking my opinions into my stories all those years apparently hadn't been without some lingering effects.

Laying out the page consisted of choosing letters to the editor, a cartoon, and columns by syndicated columnists, and arranging them and the editorials on a mockup known a "dummy" page in a visually attractive way. The people in the composing room used the dummy as a guide to create the actual page that would go to press. I worked long hours, struggled mightily, learned a lot. With the possible exception of his wife, no one was happier to see Ken return from vacation.

Less than a year later, he called me into his office to say he was quitting.

"I've been here ten years, and I believe in changing careers every ten years," he said.

With that he resigned, ran for the state legislature, and was elected. I applied for his job, but it was given to a newcomer at the paper. The reason, I later learned, was that the new guy had given the correct answer to a question during our interviews about who should be the state's next governor. My choice was a progressive, Democratic legislator. The other candidate gave the answer the bosses wanted to hear, naming a conservative Republican legislator. It's an understatement to say that Idaho is conservative. Its governor, all of its congressional representatives, and 83 of its 104 state legislators are, as of this writing, Republicans. Some of its legislators are so wildly far to the right that they appear to have shed the bonds of reality.

Robison's departure, which left me temporarily in charge of the editorial page, was but a taste of things to come. Editorial page editors came and went over the next few years, leaving me to take up the slack between editors. The time that a position was left unfilled was, in company jargon, dark time. Gannett liked dark time because it cut costs. Executives who cut costs got bonuses. One of the dark times between editorial page editors lasted several months. Twelve- to sixteen-hour days were the rule. I worked seven days a week and on a few of the most demanding days slept on the couch in the editorial page editor's office. I was there so late and had to be back so early that it wouldn't have made sense to go home. When a new editor was hired, the company thanked me for the long days and weeks by giving me $150 bonus. The annual Christmas bonus, which all employees received, was five dollars.

At Gannett headquarters, the money flowed more freely. A friend who worked there after working at *The Statesman* told of ethnic menus in the cafeteria and company president Al Neuharth scattering Godiva chocolates on a carpet beneath the backside of a sheep sculpture.

Gannett executives were not noted for kindness to their underlings. Every few years, the company sent a team of its top executives to *The Statesman* to meet with its publisher and editors. I was within earshot when our political editor gamely tried to interview Neuharth, who responded to questions by saying "That's a really stupid question," or "That's the dumbest question I've ever heard."

During one of my stints as acting editorial page editor, I was invited to join *The Statesman*'s publisher, its editors and the corporate VIPs for a country club lunch during one of the team's visits. The senior member of the team was John Quinn, who went on to become a Gannett president. I was shocked when, during what had previously been a pleasant, poolside lunch, he viciously tore into the publisher, embarrassing him in front of his employees.

It was Quinn who, years later, led a campaign for Gannett newspapers to include minority sources in stories. Our computers were programmed so that stories couldn't be written without first completing a form on which minority sources had to be listed. Mainstreaming, the company's term for including minorities, was a laudable goal, but the results were sometimes ludicrous. Boise is an overwhelmingly white city, and it was even more so in those days. Desperate to include nonwhite sources, reporters tended to use the same ones over and over, sometimes quoting them in stories about subjects in which they had neither expertise nor interest—a fact that escaped neither them nor writers of caustic letters to the editor.

Rude behavior like Quinn's and Neuharth's was, if not standard procedure for Gannett executives, hardly uncommon. When the team came to town led by a subsequent Gannett president, he insulted the corporation's head of advertising, a former *Statesman* publisher, in front of a room full of coworkers over dinner. My friend who worked at Gannett headquarters told a story of a top executive giving orders to deny promotions to a colleague who questioned one of his statements during a staff meeting. If I had to come up with the word that best described the Gannett corporate culture in those days, it would be mean.

It was a big deal in Idaho when native son Frank Church, a United States senator, ran for president. I helped cover his announcement ceremony and, like most Idahoans, followed his campaign with interest. Church's biggest mistake was entering the race too late. Jimmy Carter had already built a formidable lead. Church tried to make light of his "late, late strategy" by wearing a tie with turtles on it. He won several primaries, but was too late to stop the Carter juggernaut. After bowing out, he agreed to be interviewed about his campaign by *The Statesman's* editorial board. The interview was conducted in the publisher's office.

"Tim, you know Senator Church," the publisher said as we gathered to shake hands.

"Of course!" I said, reaching out to shake the hand of the most famous man in the state—and spilling the coffee the senator had just accepted from the publisher's secretary. Scalding hot, it found its way into his shoe. With agility belying the turtle strategy, he frantically hopped around the room on one foot while trying to pry the shoe off of the other one.

Mortified, I all but prostrated myself apologizing.

Church was as nice as he was famous. He laughed and said it could have happened to anyone.

A few weeks later, Carter came to town. His only stop was a brief one at the airport. A photographer and I were assigned the story. The television stations each were given two minutes with Carter. *The Statesman*, for a reason we never knew, was given none. When Carter and his entourage left without a word to the print media, the photographer and I were left waiting in a concourse, feeling rebuffed and desperate.

Then, a miracle. Carter's press secretary emerged from an office door, heading straight for us.

"Sorry about the mixup," he said. "We have plane trouble. How would you guys like forty minutes with the next president of the United States?"

We interviewed him in the airport manager's office. Carter was relaxed and friendly. He patiently answered our questions without being evasive or confrontational, a rarity for a politician. My story was okay, but the photographer's picture was better. It was of Carter leaning back in the airport manager's chair, his feet up on a desk next to a sign reading, "Don Duvall, Airport Manager."

Carter proved to be a better ex-president than president, devoting himself well into his nineties to helping the underprivileged. Would Church have been a better president? My guess is that he would have. Unlike Carter, whose highest previous political office had been governor of Georgia, Church had been elected three times to the U.S. Senate, helped pass the Civil Rights Act, served as chairman of the Senate's Foreign Relations Committee, and had investigated abuses within the intelligence community. Like Carter, he also was a principled, decent man—qualities that should be essential for anyone aspiring to be president.

My proudest achievement as acting editorial page editor was adding Mike Royko to *The Statesman*'s lineup of syndicated columnists. A Chicago columnist, Royko had long been one of my favorites. He wrote like no one else—brilliant, acerbic, witheringly funny. One of his columns criticized columnist George Will for his cozy relationship with President Ronald Reagan, which was reflected in Will's columns. Royko wrote that journalism's most important role is that of the watchdog, but in Will's relationship with Reagan it more closely resembled that of a lap dog. I was able to get Royko's column for a reasonable fee, but failed in my attempt to add one of my other favorite columnists to the page.

Russell Baker was as good a wordsmith as Royko, but in a gentler way. A two-time Pulitzer Prize winner, he was an institution at *The New York Times*. When my time as acting editorial page editor ended, the executive editor suggested that I write a column about my time as acting editorial page editor. In it, I mentioned my disappointment at being unable to get Baker's column.

A few weeks later, a letter arrived in an elegant, cream-colored envelope printed with *The New York Times* return address. It was from Baker, who said he'd read my column and thanked me for trying to get his.

"Unfortunately, you'd have to have bought the entire *Times* wire to do that," he wrote. "If you'd done that, it would have raised my standing around here enough to get me a $10 raise."

He went on to write that he had discovered a marvelous letter from Mark Twain to Harvard University, which had offered him an honorary degree. Baker's letter quoted Twain's:

"Thank you for offering me an honorary degree, but when I was a struggling, unknown writer I didn't see Harvard coming around with any degrees. And now that I have one from Oxford, I have no need of one from second-line universities."

Royko, Baker, and Mark Twain were my kind of writers. Compared with what they did, writing editorials about the city council, the school board, or the mosquito abatement district was tedious. I wanted to write more personally, about things that interested me and would interest readers who weren't hard-news junkies.

But how? By this time I had worked as a feature writer, government reporter, investigative reporter, general assignment reporter, editorial writer, and acting editorial page editor. All had had their moments, but none was what I wanted to do for life. What if any newspaper job could give me lasting fulfillment? What would be my niche, if there even was one?

The paper's new editor knew the answer to that before I did.

CHAPTER NINE
'I Saw the Future Coming'

No one who was there will forget the day Dick Hronek's career went off the rails.

Hronek had been a good newspaperman. He was smart, had a solid background as a reporter and editor, and was a fine writer. He was not, however, a people person. He was reserved, withdrawn. While the newsroom buzzed with activity, he'd sit alone in his office with the shades drawn. This did not sit well with a staff of outgoing journalists. Instead of a dynamic, outgoing leader, we had a virtual hermit in charge.

It was an unusually quiet afternoon in the newsroom when he emerged from his office carrying a box of his personal belongings. The reporter at the desk next to mine tried to make light of it.

"What's the matter, Dick? Can't you take it any more?"

He stopped and solemnly stared at her, considering his response.

"No, Mindy," he said after a long pause. "I guess I can't."

We never saw him again, never were given the precise reason for his departure.

His replacement, the editor who knew my niche in the newspaper world before I did, was almost his exact opposite. Gary Watson had arrived not long before as the news editor, the number two job in the newsroom. A generation younger, Watson was the kind of leader we needed—dynamic, smart, committed to improving the newspaper and, not coincidentally, his odds of rising within the Gannett Company.

Not long after getting the job, he invited me to lunch. It was obvious, to me at least, that the reason was a letter I'd written to the publisher the day before about the editorial page editor's job being given to a newcomer after I'd spent months doing it.

"I hear you were upset about not getting the editorial page editor's job," Watson said over lunch.

"The publisher must have shown you my letter."

"No," he replied, all innocence. "What letter?"

I was all but certain that he was lying. That he would take me to lunch to discuss my career goals without having seen the letter given to the publisher a day before was unlikely at best.

"My letter to the publisher," I replied. "It said what you just said—that I was upset about not getting the job."

"I didn't know that, but I can understand why you wouldn't have been happy about it. Here's the thing, though. I don't think you want to be a paper pusher. The editorial page editor's job is a lot of detail, a lot of paperwork. You're a writer, not a paper pusher. You've shown that with the things you've written. How would you like to try writing a column?"

The instant the words left his lips, I saw the future coming. A column would be perfect. It would allow me to express my opinions, free from the dictates of editorial writing and straight reporting. It would let me write personally and, when appropriate, with humor.

"We'll start out with one column a week," Watson said. "If that goes well, we'll increase the frequency."

I left the restaurant that day walking six inches off the ground. All that was needed was to prove that I deserved the opportunity.

My first few columns were anything but humorous. The only explanation for their somber tone and grim subject matter that makes sense to me now was that I was trying to impress my coworkers, the serious reporters who lived to write about the machinations of government. They rightly saw government reporting and investigative reporting as journalism's highest calling. Anything else they considered second rate. Already feeling like somewhat of an outsider because of their cool reactions to my front-page feature stories, I didn't want them to think I'd be writing fluff columns.

My first, published on September 14, 1975, was about a fourteen-year-old alcoholic. "Jody," a fictitious name used to conceal his identity, grew up with no father and an alcoholic mother. The column attributed his drinking to that and to the tenor of the times:

"On a recent day, the president was almost shot by a woman who claimed to worship a convicted mass murderer. A bomb planted for political reasons killed two bystanders and injured forty-nine others in London .... A town abolished Halloween after poison and razor blades were planted in treats. The number of marriages and divorces in the newspaper that day were equal.

"Half a million Jodys may be among the results."

And a cheery Top 'o the Mornin' to you, *Statesman* readers.

Another early effort was about the passing of a homeless man:

"The old man was lowered in a cheap, cloth-covered casket into a nondescript burial box identified only as space five, section twenty-five, block eight of the Valley View Cemetery District. There were no flowers, no prayers, no headstone. The county paid for what little there was, the casket and the hole in the ground. Soon the scarred earth will heal. There will be nothing left to mark the passing of Wallace Christensen."

No one attended Mr. Christensen's funeral. Since no one else seemed to care, I did some research and reported what details could be found about his life. He and I had attended the same high school, though in different generations. He'd been married three times, had children. He drank heavily. He was said to have been smart and witty, "a bum of his own choosing."

Lightening up a bit, I changed gears by covering "The Lowman Burping Contest." Lowman is a mountain community of some twenty-five year-round residents about an hour's drive from Boise—in good weather. In the winter on icy roads, it can take twice that long. The burping contest was held in the bar of the lodge there and was good not only for a humor column but one about the trip home. "Driving Through Woods on a Snowy Evening" described the white-knuckle drive, on slick roads over two mountain passes, and my fear of possibly not making it home.

"The temperature in town is near zero tonight. Here, it's colder .... I try to remember how long a person in city clothes can survive subzero cold. The beauty of the night is lost now. The Christmas-card pines become Tolkien monsters, eerie and grotesque in the shifting beam of the headlights.

"You think all sorts of things at such a time. ... Your preferences on dying. (They do not include freezing.) Your life. How good or bad it has been. Your preference for hanging on to it."

Safely home, the snowy passes behind, "I sigh hugely and look at my watch. One o'clock in the morning. The neighborhood is dark, silent, incredibly lovely."

Or so it seemed. One of the reasons I remember that particular column when so many others are forgotten was the date of that night drive—December 8, 1980. Expecting to find the family asleep when I shut off the engine and crept inside the house, I was surprised to find Sheila awake and in tears. My first thought was that something terrible had happened to one of the children. It was almost a relief when she explained the reason for her tears. While I was negotiating mountain roads, John Lennon had been murdered.

As is the case with many tragic events, it took time to feel the full impact. Along with the rest of the Beatles, Lennon had been as much of a force in our lives as if we had known him personally. The Beatles changed the way we looked, the music we played, the way we thought. They had been our heroes, and the loss of the charismatic John Lennon was as painful as it was surreal. Watching crowds of thousands mourning him on television the next day made it worse. The surreal became real, the grief a wound to an entire generation.

Gannett, meanwhile, was growing, expanding its empire. Already the nation's largest newspaper chain, it had its sights set on bigger things than local newspapers. I'd been a columnist for seven years when, in the summer of 1982, Watson left for a corporate meeting in Seattle. This had never happened before, and the staff was itching to know what the meeting was about and what was decided there.

We didn't have to wait long. The day after returning home, Watson called a staff meeting. I'm paraphrasing, but this is reasonably close to what he said that day:

"From now on, we're going to be almost entirely local. The company wants us to be the voice of our communities. We'll still report some national news, but not nearly as much and unless it's a really huge story it won't be on the front page any more. From now on, it's all about being local."

This was a huge change. *The Statesman* for as long as I could remember had run national and world news on its front pages. Only the most outstanding local stories were deemed worthy of Page One. Now it would be local stories, some of little import, on the front page, with an anemic smattering of world and national news buried inside.

It wasn't long before we knew why. Gannett was reducing local competition for national and international news in the cities where it owned newspapers. This would improve the odds of success for its new national newspaper. *USA Today* debuted within a few weeks.

Returning from a vacation in the Seattle area, where I'd been reading national and international news on the front page of *The Seattle Times*, I was struck by how shallow the local-only policy sometimes made *The Statesman* seem. The banner headline of the lead story on *The Statesman's* front page: "Citizens Band Radio Craze Hits Boise."

By then, Gannett had become tight-fisted with respect to the budgets of its local newspapers. Gone were the days of traveling to England to chase ghosts or riding the rails around the country to do a story a day. It was clear how much things had changed when I put in a request to go to McCall, a two-hour drive from Boise, to cover a story there. It would have been up and back the same day, the only expenses being my mileage and lunch. The request was denied for lack of travel money.

Sheila's and my life changed forever in 1975, the year I became a columnist. Our first child arrived that January. The doctor said the baby would be born around Christmas so we named her Andrea Noelle. She was born January 28. Our second daughter, Jennifer, was born the following year.

A disproportionate number of our vacations with the girls had a way of becoming minor disasters. We pitched our tent in the middle of the night on a red-ant hill. Our Coleman camp stove exploded. The kids invariably waited until we left on vacations to get sick. We were unpacking at Sheila's folks' cabin when Jenny, still in diapers, crawled to a dog dish with a residue of scummy water and lapped it up, triggering diarrhea of shocking proportions. Her sister responded by vomiting prodigiously on the cloth upholstery of our in-laws' new car.

Before leaving on a trip to Glacier National Park, the kids came down with chicken pox. They were pretty much over them by the time we left, but the episode left me with a decidedly uneasy feeling.

"Have I ever had chicken pox?" I asked my mother.

"Let's see. You had mumps, you had measles. ... No, I don't remember that you ever had chicken pox."

I woke up with them in Kalispell, Montana, a day after leaving Glacier National Park, and was sick for the duration of the trip. The silver lining, as it so often is with such adversities, was a ready-made column subject:

"There is a numbing sameness to these bedridden days. Those in the know have gone out of their way to tell me that chicken pox is much harder on adults than on children, a theory I am in no position to dispute. I have 171 pock marks on my chest and stomach, 126 on my face. They're in my ears, my nose, my mouth. I can't shave or brush my teeth without a blood transfusion …. I am the world's ugliest human. By comparison, Lon Chaney, the Elephant man, and Quasimodo are radiant beauties."

Sickness dogged us to an almost unbelievable degree during vacations with the kids. To save money on motels for one particularly memorable trip, I installed hangers for a makeshift hammock to stretch from one side of our Volkswagen bus to the other, above the front seats. This was to be Jennifer's bed. She would have been three or four then. Sheila and I and Andie, then five, would sleep on a mattress in the back of the bus.

Early in the trip, both of the girls caught colds. My strongest memory of that vacation is of being up all night in a freezing campground on the Oregon Coast, listening to the kids cough, sneeze, and wail piteously. We decided to cut the trip short and come home early, having had as much vacation as we could stand. On our way home, the VW's generator failed, draining the battery. When we stopped for gas or bathroom breaks, we had to park it on an incline and let it coast downhill until it was rolling fast enough to pop the clutch to start the engine. By the time we reached the pass over the Blue Mountains, it was nearly dark. With no generator and thus no headlights, we had to park for the night on a hill in a rest stop at a place appropriately named Deadman Pass. I've driven past there many times since, and the memory of the four of us squeezed into that van, fighting colds and hypothermia during one of the longest nights of our lives, remains fresh as if it had happened last week.

For Christmas one year, we splurged and bought plane tickets to Seattle for a holiday visit with relatives in Olympia, Washington. When we arrived at the airport in Boise for our evening flight, we were told that Seattle was fogged in and our flight had been canceled. We were rebooked for the first flight out the following morning.

"No problem," I naively said. "We'll go home, get a good night's sleep and be in Olympia for lunch tomorrow."

Morning came with Seattle still shut down. We waited for the next flight, also canceled. Given the option of flying to fog-free Portland, we eagerly accepted. Portland had more Seattle flights than Boise did, improving the odds of getting there once the weather cleared.

The fog, however, was relentless. It continued to keep Seattle's airport closed while we spent the afternoon trying to keep our energetic toddlers under control in Portland's airport, which was teeming with hundreds of stranded passengers. When the airline offered Seattle-bound passengers the option of taking a bus, accepting the offer seemed like a no brainer. By then, we'd have taken a rickshaw to Seattle.

A rickshaw might have been faster. The bus, an ancient yellow school bus, broke down a few miles south of Olympia.

"Just let us out here," we said to the driver. "Our relatives live in Olympia. They can come and pick us up."

"Sorry, can't do that. I have to take you to Sea-Tac airport. Regulations."

By the time the bus was repaired and we arrived at Sea-Tac, enough time had passed since our original departure time that we could have driven to Seattle and back. Then we had to wait for Sheila's mother to come from Olympia, an hour away, to pick us up. For reasons that were never clear, she brought her poodle and Jake, her octogenarian father, along. While we were loading the luggage into the trunk, the poodle stepped on a button on the console, locking the doors with the key inside. That triggered the car alarm, which in turn set Jake's hearing aids to howling. Between him walking around slapping his ears, the alarm blaring, and a cop screaming at us about being parked in a no-parking zone, we didn't know whether to laugh or shoot ourselves.

The following Christmas, having had our fill of holiday flying, we took the train. Long since discontinued, Amtrak's Pioneer Route from Denver to Seattle had stops in Boise and Olympia. Taking the train was the best decision we could have made. Fog once again had closed the airports, and a snowstorm had closed the pass over the Blue Mountains. The train literally was the only way to get to our destination. We played cards and board games in the dining car and enjoyed picture-perfect snowscapes while the train negotiated the silent pass, deep in fresh snow. It was our best trip to date.

It was, that is, until a relative arrived for Christmas Eve at Sheila's parents' house and announced that her kids "seem to have picked up a little cold." This would have been Christmas 1985. Mark, our third and last child, had just turned three. By New Year's, all five of us as well as Sheila's folks had the cold from hell. We were up all night coughing for weeks. It was spring before we all were well again.

My illnesses—colds, flu, chicken pox—so reliably coincided with our vacations that at a newsroom Christmas party one year the editors presented me with a distinguished service award for "selflessly saving up sick time for vacations." My vacations provided so much story material that they were one of the two things I was best known for during my early years as a columnist.

The other was Maintenance Manor.

Maintenance Manor, as it came to be called after establishing itself as a column staple, was an old house in Boise's North End. It was roughly eighty years old when we bought it, in what had to have been one of the most foolishly optimistic decisions of our lives.

It wasn't a fixer-upper—it was a nightmare. The porch and floors sagged. The wiring needed to be replaced, the plumbing dated to the late nineteenth century, and the one bathroom could be reached only from a closet and the back porch. The back porch had sheets of flapping, translucent plastic instead of windows. The woodwork was painted black. The living-room carpet was pea-soup green and hideous even before the former owners endowed it with dozens of cigarette burns. The basement resembled nothing so much as a dungeon. It was home to an ancient furnace that guzzled oil at such an alarming rate that the heating-oil company ranked the house among the half dozen least efficient in its customer base. There was no garage, no insulation, no square corners. The roof needed replacing; the chimney was crumbling. And even if it had been in good condition with none of these deficiencies, the house was ugly.

Why did we buy it? We put our trust in the real estate bromide—location, location, location. Ghastly as it was, the house was in a beautiful neighborhood of well-maintained older homes on a street shaded by stately trees. We paid $20,000 for it, never dreaming that it would cost that much and more to make it a home where we'd be comfortable living.

For a number of reasons, not the least of which was that her father was a skilled handyman, we invited Sheila's folks to drive from Olympia to visit and see the house, hinting that it would be nice if he brought along some of his tools.

Their initial reaction was stunned silence. Sheila's mother was the first to speak:

"Nothing you could have said would have prepared me for this. If you said you had bought a shell … No, even that wouldn't have prepared me."

Sheila's father kept his opinion to himself until he had walked around the house and yard, methodically inspecting the foundation, the roof, and each of the rooms.

"What do you think, John?" I asked him.

He weighed his words.

"… Well, it is a nice neighborhood. If it were my house, I'd tear it down and build a new house on the lot."

It proved to be the best advice we ever ignored. Numerous home buyers since then have torn down old North End homes and built new ones in their place. We, on the other hand, spent the next thirteen years waging war with the old house that ate the young couple.

For the opening campaign of the war, we enlisted the aid of Sheila's father, my father, a retired homebuilder who offered to help for free, an elderly carpenter who worked by the hour, a plumber, and an electrician.

The plumber was the fourth one we tried to hire, the first three having taken one look at the place and turned us down flat. The fourth agreed to replumb the house only because it had a clawfoot bathtub in a style he'd been looking for and would do the job if we gave it to him as partial payment.

We learned from the electrician not to pay anyone in advance. Paid in full, he vanished with the job half finished and stole one of our wedding gifts, a set of Italian crystal, for good measure.

The retired homebuilder threw in the towel after a couple of days, saying he'd underestimated the amount of work.

"It could take the rest of my life and we still wouldn't be finished," he said.

Then in his eighties, he died years before we were finished.

The carpenter quit after a few days.

Sheila's folks left town after a few days.

We were on our own.

The travails of the next thirteen years are too numerous to mention, but a few episodes stand out:

—Watching from the attic as a beam I was sawing gave way and crashed into the kitchen, missing my father by inches. It was heavy enough that it could have killed him.

—Trying everything from paint remover to a belt sander to a propane torch in futile attempts to strip the gummy black paint off of the woodwork. I ended up having to make new woodwork for the entire house.

—Falling from the roof while attempting to repair the chimney, my landing cushioned by a rose bush.

—Staying up until the small hours hanging wallpaper in the new bathroom, the one we built to replace the one accessible only from the back porch and closet. When we woke up the next morning, the wallpaper hung with such difficulty was lying in a soggy mess on the floor.

—The wrong color of Formica being delivered for the kitchen counter, resulting in a ten-day delay in installing the sink and dishes having to be washed in the bathtub. One of the lowest moments was coming home after a hard day's work to find bits of lettuce clinging to the sides of the tub.

—Switching on the family room ceiling fan, which I'd just installed and oiled, and watching in horror as oil splattered the new wallpaper and carpet like rounds from a gatling gun.

—Carefully cutting a two-and-one-quarter-inch hole in the new front door and watching the dead bolt I was trying to install fall through the hole. (It was supposed to have been a two-and-one-eighth-inch hole.) I was so infuriated that I picked up the deadbolt and threw it as hard as I could.

Through a window of the VW bus.

—Our toddler daughter tapping a wall with my hammer and saying "dammit, dammit, dammit."

"Where did you learn that word?" Sheila asked her.

"From Daddy."

I was taking a break one summer afternoon when a group of people with tennis rackets rode by on bicycles and jauntily waved. I'd been working on the house since dawn and was exhausted, frustrated, and covered with drywall taping mud. That moment more than any other made me realize how much Maintenance Manor was costing in time that could never be salvaged.

Most people would have taken that as a sign to finish the house as quickly as possible, sell it for a nice profit, and move to a home where these sorts of things didn't happen. Most people, but not us. Instead of moving on, we added on: a family room, bathroom, and home office. We prudently hired an architect to design the addition and a contractor to do most of the heavy lifting. All I had to do was paint, hang wallpaper, make woodwork to match the rest of the house, install the aforementioned ceiling fan, lay some bricks in the entryway, pour the concrete for the back step, and a few other minor projects.

With the addition finished, we liberated ourselves at long last by selling the place. I was nailing up the last piece of molding while the realtor put up the "For Sale" and "Open House" signs in the front yard. Thirteen years after purchasing the place for $20,000, we sold it for $70,000. Subtracting the costs of materials and professional labor, our sweat equity was worth pennies an hour.

This was just before the boom that saw the value of North End homes skyrocket. A few years later, with its next owners having done virtually nothing to the house, it sold for $120,000. It subsequently sold again for roughly double that amount. Its estimated value on zillow.com at the time of this writing is $673,000. It's been extensively remodeled, but still ….

Location—and timing—are everything in real estate.

Though I wrote enough columns about Maintenance Manor and travel mishaps that readers identified me as "that guy who writes about vacation and home remodeling disasters," they actually comprised a small fraction of my output. Watson increased the frequency of my columns from one a week to two and then three. I wrote three a week for eighteen years, along with occasional news and feature stories and special projects.

There was enough positive input from readers in the form of letters, phone calls, and personal contacts that in 1981, having six years' worth of columns under my belt, I decided to publish some of the best as a book. *The Statesman* agreed to give me the copyrights, and I chose the Caxton Printers, Ltd., based in Caldwell, Idaho, to do the printing. Financially, it was a gamble. I'd be paying the printing costs out of my own pocket and had zero experience in the book business. The good news was that there were nearly a dozen independent book stores in Boise (there is one now), and their owners were willing to sell the books with a 20 percent discount, meaning I'd get 80 percent of the cover price. *The Statesman* helped by promoting the books, and I kept costs down by delivering them to the stores myself, loading cases of them into the trunk of my car, and lugging them down streets and alleys to the shops that would sell them. If there is anything heavier per square foot than books, I don't know what it is. Lead, perhaps.

My fear that they might not sell was put to rest with the first autograph signing, at The Book Shop in downtown Boise. Now a wistful memory, it was Idaho's oldest and most comprehensive book store. The first printing of *Shirttail Journalist* (I considered myself a shirttail relative of the real thing) sold out in a few days and went through two additional printings. Four more column collections followed. The books helped pay for Maintenance Manor repairs and other expenses. The payoff that meant most, however, was the connection with the readers. Book signings were a way to meet them in person, listen to their stories, and put faces with the names.

Life doesn't seem as funny to me as it once did, but early on I wrote a lot of humor columns. Subjects ranged from the challenges of modern life to incidents in my own life to absurdities gleaned from the headlines:

Shopping for stereos in stores where I didn't understand a word of the salesmen's

In *The Statesman* newsroom. Hundreds of Tim's columns and stories were written at this desk.

technological babble. The challenges of procuring normal clothing during the disco era. A rogue wave swallowing my wallet and Tourist ID Card (required for reentry to the U.S.) on a beach in Mexico. Congressmen who looked like Elmer Fudd, a club for people who were too good-looking, the Montana Merchant Marine ....

The most widely reprinted of my columns ran with a one-word headline, "Idaho."

An excerpt:

"Idaho is a million-dollar home with a view of the skyline, a baby crying in the hopelessness of a migrant labor camp. Idaho is a general store with everything in the midst of nothing, a restaurant that serves eight kinds of homemade pie in the middle of nowhere. Idaho is wilderness: jade lakes in granite basins, stories around the campfire, hot springs under the stars. It's huckleberries and hummingbirds and hunters in the hills. Raptors and rookeries and rivers on the run.

"… Other states have beckoned, but the sum of their offers is at best a trade. When you're tired of Idaho, you're tired of life."

For a long time, I thought "Idaho" was the best thing I'd ever written. Now it's hard to say. It was written in 1982, a lot of years ago, a lot of words ago. But if nothing else, it was a reasonably accurate snapshot of the state as it existed then. Now, with its population doubled and changes that have made parts of it almost unrecognizable, Idaho is a different and in some ways a lesser place. I'm glad I wrote "Idaho" when I did.

Christmas Eve 1987 brought one of those phone calls you don't forget. We were spending the holidays with Sheila's folks in Olympia at the time.

"It's for you," Sheila said.

"Me? Who would be calling me here on Christmas Eve?"

"It's Rod Sandeen."

Sandeen was *The Statesman*'s managing editor, a no-nonsense newsman. A call from him during a vacation, let alone on Christmas Eve, couldn't be good news. He was calling to tell me that Jim Poore, the sports editor and a good friend, had suffered what originally was thought to have been a stroke.

"I didn't want you to find out by reading it in the newspaper," Sandeen said.

Jim was only forty-two. Because he couldn't have cared less about details—he put bills in his trash compacter and went three years without filing a tax return—I'd occasionally encouraged him to speak with a financial advisor. His response was always the same.

"Why should I do that? I'll never see fifty."

He thought his failure to lose weight would lead to a fatal stroke or heart attack. He never figured on a cerebral aneurysm. It left him in a coma for two years before he died.

That Christmas Eve was the last time I ever spoke to Sandeen. When I returned from vacation, he was gone, transferred to another Gannett job and replaced by someone who could not have been more different. Unlike Sandeen the hard-core newsman, the new editor was more of a soft-news type. His idea of responding to a major national news story was to send reporters to the mall to do "man on the street" interviews. No story was to be longer than ten inches, providing about as much depth as a wading pool. His nickname was "Captain Breakout," after his penchant for breaking a few sentences or paragraphs out of an already short story and running them in a box with a separate headline. His tenure was brief.

His replacement was an excellent newsman, but a force to be feared as much as respected. Formerly an editor at the *Saint Petersburg Times*, he taught us to think big. When I was working on a story commemorating the tenth anniversary of U.S. Senator Frank Church's death, he read it and told me to get a quote from Senator Edward Kennedy. This would not have occurred to me. We were accustomed to relying on Idaho sources, not national luminaries. Kennedy didn't return any of my repeated calls, but I did get a quote from former Senate Majority Leader Mike Mansfield.

The new editor made *The Statesman* a more exciting place to work, but it was scarier as well. He had a predilection for firing people who displeased him, which wasn't hard to do. The first casualty was a friend and fellow columnist. In his first week on the job, the new boss took her column away from her. It was the part of the job she loved best, so she quit.

Other resignations or firings followed at a steady pace. The most traumatic case was that of a sportswriter who was recruited from a paper in his home state of Texas because the boss liked his writing. He was hired as a sports columnist, but upon arriving was congratulated on becoming the new sports editor, a job involving far more editing and supervising than writing. It was too late for him to back out because he'd quit his former job and moved his family to Boise. He stuck it out for a couple of years, during which the boss increasingly criticized his work and generally made his life miserable. He eventually quit and moved back to Texas. He was a good writer and a good man who deserved better than the way he was treated in Boise. Or, as he called it, "Failureville."

Another of the victims was a former features editor who filled in as the executive editor until the arrival of the aforementioned boss, who promptly demoted him to religion reporter. He made his life as religion reporter so stressful that he came up with an ingenious way to avoid quitting or being fired. He got his doctor to write a note saying that he was to stay home indefinitely because the environment in which he was forced to work was lethal to his health. He stayed home until the boss backed off and agreed to treat him better.

When the boss invited me to lunch one day, I was certain that he was going to fire me. The real reason for the invitation proved to be a pleasant surprise. The political columnist was about to leave for a year's fellowship, and I was asked over Moon's Cafe sandwiches to write more columns in his absence.

The pleasure was short-lived. The boss left for a job in a neighboring state, and his replacement cut the frequency of my columns and changed the day of the week that my one remaining column would run. After eighteen years of writing a Sunday column, I learned that I'd no longer be in the Sunday paper from reading about it in her Sunday column.

Years later, shortly after retiring from *The Statesman*, I met a former colleague at a sports bar to watch a Cubs game. Over a beer, he told me something that should have been obvious but had never occurred to me.

"I thought you handled the resentment well," he said.

"Resentment? What resentment?"

"The editors resentment of your column."

"I didn't know they did resent it. What do you mean?"

He seemed surprised.

"You didn't know?"

"No. I have no idea what you're talking about."

"They resented the popularity of your column. They'd spend weeks planning and editing one of their big projects, it would run on the Sunday front page, and on Monday readers would tell them how much they liked your Sunday column. They hated that."

Suddenly some things made sense: Not telling me in person that my Sunday column had been canceled. Making me work the Sunday shift, normally reserved for rookies, when I was one of the most senior staff members. Not once in forty years giving me an Employee of the Month Award.

Am I bitter about that?

For a long time, yes.

But not any more. Life's too short.

For much of the time I worked there, newsroom morale was pretty low. But there also were times when *The Statesman*'s publishers and editors (Bob Miller, Gary Watson, Rod Sandeen, Vicki Gowler, and Mi-Ai Parrish come to mind) made it a pretty good and occasionally fun place to work. And for me, most of the work itself was a joy. If they hadn't paid me for it, I almost would have done it for free.

The key word in that sentence being "almost."

CHAPTER TEN
Memorable Assignments

C olumns have been my stock in trade, but many assignments had nothing to do with writing columns.

When a fire broke out in the mountains near Boise one afternoon, all of the reporters were out of the newsroom on other assignments. The managing editor emerged from her office to summon her staff and, seeing only me, had me head for the hills. Stuart Wong, the only photographer around at the time, was the other half of the team.

Covering a forest fire is a little like the way airline pilots describe their job: hours of boredom punctuated by moments of panic. Most of covering a wildfire involves waiting around for the boss of the fire crew to give you updates. That often means that you're nowhere near the fire itself, partly for your own safety. For reporters, this makes it challenging to write anything descriptive. For photographers, it's anathema. Without a fire to photograph, they're limited to shots of weary firefighters milling around during their breaks or, worse, sleeping.

Arriving on the scene, we were told that a ranch house was in the fire's path and in danger of being lost. We couldn't see the house, let alone the fire, because we were told to wait by my car, parked on a dirt road a few hundred yards away.

This did not sit well with Stuart, who, eager to get a photograph of firefighters protecting the ranch house, walked up the road to be closer to the action. I accompanied him. We were in view of the house when he happened to glance back down the road.

"Oh, shit!"

This was not a casual pronouncement, as in "Oh, shit; they won't let us go up there." It was an "Oh, shit; run for your life!" In the few minutes it had taken us to walk up the road, the wind had changed and the fire was roaring down the mountainside between us and my car. The sound, the smoke, the heat, the primal force of the fire were terrifying. We had seconds before it cut us off from the car or, worse, transformed the car into a cinder.

Few people in the history of forest fires have run faster. We felt the fire's fury in every pore as we raced past it, almost through it, to get to the car and back it up to a safer place.

We didn't get much of a story that day, a few paragraphs about the house being saved, an update on containment efforts, some pictures of weary firefighters.

Which was okay. We were grateful just to have made it home safely.

When word came that eastern Idaho's Teton Dam had collapsed on a Saturday morning in June 1975, it wasn't long before my phone rang with orders to report for duty.

The Teton Dam failure was a huge story that I initially underestimated. It wasn't as if the dam was in a heavily populated area. If Lucky Peak Dam, a few miles above Boise, had failed, it would have made headlines worldwide. Thousands of people would have died. But Teton Dam, a relatively small, earthen dam in a lightly populated part of eastern Idaho? How big a story could that be?

I had no idea.

My first view of the floodwaters was in Idaho Falls. Even there, the Snake River was all but unrecognizable. Normally a modest channel with a picturesque waterfall near the city center, the Snake had become a broad sheet of muddy water that extended far beyond the river's usual banks. It had all but obliterated the waterfall.

Idaho Falls, more than thirty miles from the dam, had time to prepare and avoid significant damage. At Sugar City, where a *Statesman* photographer and I concentrated our efforts, it was another story. Sugar City, thirteen miles from the dam, was leveled. It was as if the hand of God had reached down and crushed it. Homes were reduced to mounds of rubble with shattered boards and shards of glass protruding from them. The valley floor was littered with fractured furniture, muddy clothing, water-logged books and photos. Poignant mementos of lives forever altered. I'll never forget the images of a little girl's doll lying in the mud or the haggard face of Anna Ballard, an elderly woman who graciously allowed us to interview her after she had lost everything.

The same thing happened when *The Statesman* sent me to Kellogg, Idaho, to interview widows of the 1972 Sunshine Mine Disaster. It was one of those assignments that make you wish you'd chosen another occupation. Ninety-one miners had perished in a fire that started deep in the mine. All those grieving widows enduring heartbreak I could only imagine, and I was supposed to knock on their doors and ask them to share it with the world?

Not a single one of them refused to talk to me. They welcomed me into their homes, answered my questions, shared their stories. Their resilience, their willingness to open their homes and their hearts to a rookie reporter who fully expected doors to slam in his face opened my eyes to how much humans can endure without losing their capacity for kindness.

One of those making the trip to Kellogg in the aftermath of the disaster was a budding politician. Steve Symms, whose family was best known for a fruit ranch, was making his first run for Congress. Never ones to miss an opportunity to get the most out of their travel dollars, the editors asked me to interview him when not interviewing the widows.

Symms was nothing if not colorful. His slogan, "Take a Bite Out of Government," was illustrated with a rendering of an apple, presumably from the Symms Fruit Ranch, with a bite prominently removed. Friendly and folksy, he was a good interview. Quotes fell from his lips like overripe fruit.

One stands out decades later.

"If I'm elected, I'll only serve two terms," he said. "I'm not going to be one of those politicians who go to Washington and get Potomac Fever."

Symms went on to serve four terms in Congress and two in the Senate. As of this writing, he was in his eighties and still in Washington, working as a lobbyist. Potomac Fever seems to have suited him.

It was my good fortune to interview a number of famous people through the years. Karl Wallenda, leader of the famous Flying Wallendas high-wire act, agreed to not one but two interviews and posed for a photo while balanced atop a log fence. Bill Kay, a circus producer and friend of his, confided that Wallenda had recently lost his balance while standing on a stool to change a light bulb. It wasn't long after that that he fell to his death while walking a wire stretched between two 10-story hotels in Puerto Rico.

I interviewed former president Gerald Ford and baseball great Henry Aaron on a golf course in Sun Valley and spent a day with Candy Loving (her real name), *Playboy* magazine's 25th Anniversary "Playmate." It was clear that she wasn't just a pretty face when a television reporter began his interview by saying "So, you're this year's bunny?"

"We're not bunnies," she replied. "We're human beings." Besides being drop-dead gorgeous, she was smart, funny, and down-to-earth, a small-town Oklahoma girl.

I went with her to a party that night at a hotel, where the guests included Clint Eastwood. Eastwood was in Boise filming a movie called *Bronco Billy*. Famous as he was, he wasn't immune to the allure of a beautiful woman and within seconds was chatting with Candy and me. The party was held in the hotel's honeymoon suite, and we were standing not far from a heart-shaped bathtub.

"Hey, Clint," a man with a camera interrupted. "Why don't the three of you hop in the bathtub and I'll take your picture."

We did (fully clothed), and the photographer snapped away. I didn't know who he was and never saw him again, but in the off chance he reads this and still has the pictures, I'd love to hear from him. How often do you get your picture taken in a bathtub with Clint Eastwood and Candy Loving?

They were far from being the only celebrities I met on the job. I interviewed *Washington Post* Publisher Katharine Graham, musicians Neil Sedaka, John Sebastian, Richard and Karen Carpenter, and Jose Feliciano; President Jimmy Carter, Grammy Award–winning singer-songwriter Jennifer Warnes, astronauts Jim Lovell and Barbara Morgan, actress Mariel Hemingway, humorist Patrick McManus, and Chicago Seven activist Tom Hayden. I questioned Ronald Reagan at a news conference, shook hands with Kurt Vonnegut and rubbed elbows—literally—with President George H. W. Bush. The memorable thing about that was that he came close enough to brush my sleeve as he walked to a podium. In my coat pocket was a pocketknife with a blade large enough that, had I been a potential assassin, it could have been lethal. It tended to lessen my faith in the security measures used to protect our presidents.

It was my dream to interview a Beatle, but it never happened. Ringo Starr canceled our lunch interview the day before it would have happened; Paul McCartney's press agent canceled my interview with him the morning of the day that one would have happened. I was able to interview one of my guitar heroes, though. Robben Ford, named one of *Musician* magazine's 100 greatest guitarists of the twentieth century, chatted with me backstage after his Boise show. When I asked him how much time he spent practicing, he said he practiced very little, that most of his musical energy was spent on composition. I briefly considered going home and smashing all my guitars.

One interview had a significant influence on my life. It was with Opal Laurel Holmes, the widow of Idaho author Vardis Fisher. Fisher wrote thirty-six books during his career, but by the 1970s all but one were largely forgotten. Fisher's *Mountain Man* was one of two books used as the basis for the 1972 film *Jeremiah Johnson*, starring Robert Redford. Holmes gave me another of Fisher's books during our interview, and it was good enough that I read several more and developed an abiding interest in Idaho's most prolific but largely forgotten author.

Fisher's books were published between 1928 and 1960. The best, in a number of critics' opinion, was a novel titled *Dark Bridwell*. I was so taken by it that on a trip to eastern Idaho I made a point of driving the dirt road along the South Fork of the Snake River to the novel's remote setting, across the river from Fisher's boyhood home. Seeing where he grew up heightened my interest in learning more about him. No Fisher biographies existed at the time, which gave me the idea of trying to write one. Over the next four years, I read everything I could find by and about Fisher, interviewed his widow, his sister, and others who had known him and toiled late and often, researching and writing the story of his turbulent life. The Caxton Printers, Ltd., published *Tiger on the Road: The Life of Vardis Fisher* in 1989. The book was a modest sales success and enjoyed mostly favorable reviews, though one reviewer dismissed it as "amateurish." For my part, I was glad just to have finished it. By then I'd had my fill of Fisher, a gifted writer but an infuriating man. He drove one of his wives to suicide, attacked critics who reviewed his books, and in one memorable incident overturned a table full of books in a fit of rage during a book signing. It was a relief to leave him in the rearview mirror.

Interviewing celebrities could be stressful. Interviewing colorful Idaho characters was a joy. One of the best things about my job was spending time with people I came to call "Idaho Originals," unique individuals who lived life on their own terms, often in lonely, out of the way places. There used to be quite a few of them in Idaho. Most came to the state from other places, seeking independent, solitary lifestyles. Now, to the best of my knowledge, all of them are gone.

Richard "Dugout Dick" Zimmerman lived in a cave in a hillside overlooking the Salmon River. He dug the cave himself with a pick, a shovel, and a pry bar, equipped it with a wood stove, a bed, a table and chairs, lanterns, and other creature comforts, and spent the rest of his life there, from age thirty-two until his death at ninety-four. He liked his first cave well enough that he dug some twenty more, renting them by the night or by the month to others who fancied the lifestyle or couldn't afford less earthy quarters. His hillside was littered with cow skulls, old tires, rusting refrigerators, and other oddments, but was uniquely picturesque. He had a verdant orchard and garden, a jury-rigged sprinkler system for watering them, and a small herd of goats. A mainstay of his diet was mush made from goat's milk, rye flour, fermented vegetables, and stinging nettles.

He looked the way one would expect a man who lived in a cave to look—leathered face, long beard, and a head of wispy, white hair topped with a battered miner's helmet. For his own entertainment and that of his guests, he played harmonica and a beat-up guitar, belting out hobo songs learned during his younger days riding the freights. In time he became something of a celebrity, interviewed by journalists from as far away as Germany and repeatedly declining invitations to appear on *The Tonight Show* with Johnny Carson. I interviewed him several times through the years and admired him more each time. He was a man living exactly as he pleased in a world largely of his own making

The hillside where he lived belonged to the Bureau of Land Management (BLM). Recognizing that he was a piece of Idaho lore, the BLM allowed him to stay rent free until he died. The bureau subsequently destroyed the caves, citing safety concerns, but helped locals erect a modest memorial commemorating his unusual life.

A covered wagon some 200 miles away on U.S. 20 near Hill City was home to another Idaho Original, cut from similar cloth. "Sunrise," real name Louis Roman, would have been right at home at a mountain-man rendezvous. He dressed in buckskins, had a beard that hadn't been trimmed in years, and wore a six-shooter the size of a pipe wrench on his hip.

He was a living landmark. Motorists en route to Sun Valley or eastern Idaho made a point of slowing down to look for him in the draw where he kept his wagon and lined the roadside with makeshift signs stating his eccentric political views. A self-styled philosopher who came to the Camas Prairie after fleeing the failed 1956 revolution in his native Hungary, he called himself Sunrise "because the sun is what wakes people up."

"We're all victims of isms," he told me.

"Isms?"

"Yes. Communism, Catholicism, Buddhism, Mormonism … You? You're probably a victim of journalism."

Sunrise died as he lived, alone in his covered wagon, leaving an empty spot in the prairie. He's been gone for nearly a quarter century, and his absence still saddens me when I pass the site of his onetime home. He and his kind made Idaho a more interesting place to live.

The same was true of "Free Press Frances Wisner," who lived in a wilderness cabin on a bank of the Salmon River. A former telephone operator from Texas, she found the solitude she craved there. Not quite a hermit, she stayed in touch with the outside world by penning a regular column, delivered to a weekly newspaper via a back-country mail plane.

Ray Arnold, the plane's pilot and himself something of a local legend, flew me to her home for an interview. Expecting a rawboned hermit in bib overalls, I was surprised to meet a dainty looking woman waiting by the airstrip, dressed in a floor-length skirt, frilly red blouse, and a matching bonnet. She went out of her way to look nice, even though there was seldom anyone around to notice.

Frances claimed to have shot eight bears in the front yard of her cabin, which was all but held up by books. Hundreds of them. She said she had read all but religious books sent by "people concerned with saving my soul." A self-reliant woman who needed only her books, her German Shepherd, and occasional visitors to be happy, she ended our visit by saying she was "one of a very few people who live exactly the way they want."

A kindred spirit, Helena Schmidt, lived in a cabin at Starveout Creek—on the Wildhorse River a peak away from No Business Basin on the edge of Hells Canyon. The cabin was built by her father, using logs he cut by hand and dragged with a team of horses. When Helena was five, she fell from a horse and broke her arm. She got back on and rode all day, alone, to the nearest doctor. She and her husband ran a cattle ranch for three decades. She roped, fed, and milked cows, bucked hay bales, drove a team of horses, ran a mowing machine. She lived alone for thirty-two years after her husband died. Distant as her neighbors were—the nearest lived seven miles away—they thought enough of her that when her cabin burned, two years before her death, they built her a new one. She died in 2000, when her car slid off of an icy switchback on the road into Hells Canyon, the nation's deepest gorge.

There was seldom a shortage of Idaho Originals to brighten my days. One of my favorites was Harold Hannebaum, Inventor Extraordinaire. As a young man, Hannebaum invented a lawnmower by cobbling together a tractor-wheel rim, washing-machine motor, hay-mower blade, and other leftover parts. He claimed that it was the world's first rotary lawnmower and was still using it in his eighties. His inventions numbered in the hundreds. The most successful, the carousel glass fireplace, made him rich. You'd never have known it, though. He and his wife, Tillie, lived modestly in their home in Bellevue, still flirting like teenagers after decades of marriage.

When Dr. Merle Wells died, historians lamented the impossibility of downloading his brain. Idaho's historian emeritus knew more about Idaho history than anyone else has or perhaps ever will. It was almost as if he lived it himself, describing historic events that happened centuries earlier as if he'd been there personally to witness and record them. He was as colorful as he was erudite, riding around Boise on a pink, girl's bicycle, wearing a yellow overcoat with a gritty streak of bicycle-wheel mud down the back.

Morley Nelson almost singlehandedly saved bald eagles from the brink of extinction. He was the driving force in creating the Idaho Snake River Birds of Prey Natural Area, later named for him, and in bringing the World Center for Birds of Prey to Idaho. I met him at a fancy dinner celebrating the center's tenth anniversary. Hoping to sit next to some regular folks, I grabbed a seat next to the old guy wearing a jacket and string tie instead of a tuxedo, not realizing that the table where he was sitting alone was the VIP table and he was the guest of honor. I spent the evening sitting between one of the world's foremost raptor experts and British actress Lynn Redgrave, regular folks both, and have seldom enjoyed an evening more. Morley and I became friends, and I never tired of hearing his stories. Infuriated by a hunter who shot at an eagle, he broke the man's rifle over his knee. He worked with celebrities from Walt Disney to Robert Redford, won a shooting match with World War II General George Patton.

Some of the other Idaho Originals who made my job a joy rather than work:

Pinto Bennett, singer-songwriter-front man for the Famous Motel Cowboys and storyteller extraordinaire. Once famous in Europe, where he drew crowds of thousands, he built a sheep wagon and lived a solitary life in it, not far from where he grew up as the son of a sheep rancher.

Esther Palmer, who refused to sell her home when the U.S. Bureau of Reclamation bought the flood-prone town of Montour and moved everyone else out for their own safety. At eighty, she kept the house and yard looking like a showplace among the decaying skeletons of the homes that surrounded it.

Milly Norstebon, who lived on a remote patch of Elmore County desert with her husband—and sixty peacocks.

Bob Ertter, the "Prairie Captain." Ertter led a double life, alternating weeks between running the tiny Camas Prairie store at Corral, Idaho, and piloting a giant oil barge on the San Francisco Bay.

Idaho used to be a magnet for such characters. Now they are memories. Spending time with them, interviewing them and writing about them, was my favorite thing about my job.

I miss doing that.

I miss them.

With the Bicentennial of the Lewis and Clark Expedition approaching, *The Statesman's* editor asked me a question that seemed to come out of left field.

"You aren't planing to retire any time soon, are you?" she asked.

Then in my mid-fifties, I'd given little thought to retirement other than as a distant prospect.

"Retire? No, not for another ten years or so."

"Good. I didn't think so, but you never know. Some people are retiring at fifty-five these days. I'm glad you aren't because we'd like you to cover the Lewis and Clark Bicentennial, and it lasts for three years."

The three-year observance featured events around the country commemorating Lewis's and Clark's role in exploring and mapping the West at the direction of President Thomas Jefferson. Photographer Katherine Jones and I were *The Statesman's* Bicentennial team. We covered the opening events at Monticello, Jefferson's Virginia home, and spent the next three years covering lesser events closer to home. We didn't work full time on the Bicentennial project; we both continued our usual routines while sandwiching in Bicentennial stories as needed. Our primary assignments were special sections on the two Idaho Indian tribes that interacted with the Corps of Discovery.

The first was the story of Sacajawea as told by members of her tribe, the Lemhi Shoshone. We made half a dozen trips to the tribe's reservation at Fort Hall, in eastern Idaho, spending countless hours over the course of a year interviewing members of the tribe about their most famous ancestor. The other special section was about the Nez

Perce Tribe. We made roughly the same number of trips to its reservation at Lapwai, in North Idaho, to interview and photograph members of that tribe. Combined, the special sections put more than 6,000 miles on Katherine' odometer.

Like many Americans, I previously hadn't spent much time with Native Americans. I knew their history as taught in white schools, knew that beginning with Christopher Columbus whites had committed genocide against the continent's original inhabitants and stolen their land. I knew that the opening of the American West was replete with stories of one broken treaty and land grab after another. Getting to know descendants of the victims and listening to their accounts of their ancestors being cheated and abused, however, made it personal. It made me ashamed of the way my people had treated theirs. Even now, countless Native Americans are treated as second-class citizens, living in poverty on land no one else wanted. Theirs is one of the most shameful chapters in our nation's history.

It took over a year to put those 6,000 miles on Katherine's car. Kim Hughes, my partner for another assignment, put nearly 3,000 miles on hers in four days. The occasion was the debut of the Idaho Passport program, which promoted tourism by encouraging people to travel to all of the state's counties and get Idaho Passports stamped there while taking in the local attractions. Our goal was to be the first to get our passports stamped in all forty-four counties. Though we missed being first by a few hours, we finished in four exhausting days—with Kim's little sister squeezed between us in a compact pickup truck. To the best of my knowledge, her sister hasn't set foot in Idaho since.

Arguably my favorite assignment ever was traveling the country by train. Gary Watson, the editor mentioned in a previous chapter, emerged from his office one day, laid a full-page Amtrak advertisement on my desk and said he wanted me to buy one of the two-week passes it was promoting. I was to see how far I could get in two weeks and write a story a day from wherever I ended up.

They were going to pay me to do this? A train buff who loves to travel? I'd have paid them.

I made it as far east as Putney, Vermont, as far south as Birmingham, Alabama. It was October, the timing perfect for New England's fall colors. Fall in Idaho is beautiful, but fall in New England is spectacular. Never would I have believed that leaves could have such vivid and varied colors: luminous yellows and golds, fiery reds, deep purples, even pink. At the inn where I stayed in Putney, a real estate brochure advertised veritable mansions on wooded acreages with trout streams for a fraction of what they would have cost in Idaho. Real estate was so cheap that I was halfway contemplating moving there until the innkeeper told me the reason it was so inexpensive was that there was almost no industry. You had to be independently wealthy or self-employed to live there.

One of the more memorable stops on the Amtrak odyssey, and the setting for the most memorable story, was Piggott, Arkansas. It was mid-afternoon by the time I stepped off of the train there, desperate to find a story in time to make my deadline. Happily, Piggott had a weekly newspaper. Laud Payne, its silver-haired editor and publisher, was killing time on a slow afternoon when I stopped by to ask for help.

"You're looking for something to write about?" he said.

"Yes, and I don't have a lot of time."

"Good. You can write about me. I'm a pretty good story."

With that he offered to take me on a tour of the town and tell me his story. Two hours later, he'd taken me to multiple businesses, parks, and government offices and was proudly showing me the town's water tower—and I still didn't have a story. My desperation must have been obvious because he abruptly changed gears.

"Let's head out to the old Pfeiffer place."

The Pfeiffer place was an imposing, two-story home with a wraparound porch atop a green hillside on the outskirts of town. It was impressive, but at first blush not a story. Noticing that I was checking my watch at increasingly frequent intervals, Mr. Payne led me down the hill to a structure that could be described as a cross between a barn and a shack.

"See the burn marks on that wall there?" he said.

"Yes?"

"I was out hunting one day when I heard someone yelling for help. I looked over and saw that this place was on fire. A man was trying to get the shutters open to throw some papers out of the upstairs window. He shouted at me to come and help, so I did."

And that was how Laud Payne helped Ernest Hemingway save the manuscript to *A Farewell to Arms*. Hemingway was then married to Pauline Pfeiffer, whose family owned the house on the hill. He was temporarily living there and working in the shack.

I had my story for that day.

When Amtrak threatened to end its Pioneer Route, which served southern Idaho, *The Statesman* had me do a story on what Idahoans could be losing. The Pioneer went from Seattle to Denver and connected with other trains that provided connections to other parts of the country. This trip was a relatively short one, from Boise to Portland to San Francisco to Salt Lake City and back to Boise. The weather was springlike in San Francisco, with flowers blooming and people dressed in summer clothes, but everywhere else it was still February. It was a shock, after leaving balmy San Francisco, to get off the train to bitter cold and more than a foot of snow in Salt Lake City.

It was early in the morning, just starting to get light, and my connection to Boise wouldn't arrive until early the next morning. At loose ends, I took a bus to Ogden in hopes of catching up with an old friend who lived there. Her home would have been a welcome refuge from the wintry weather, but no one answered when I called. I killed time at the public library until it closed and lingered as long as possible over dinner in a snug restaurant. The restaurant closed early, as just about everything else in Ogden seemed to do that night. Calls to my friend's house continued to go unanswered, so I was left to wander the streets. The temperature was well below freezing when my wandering took me to the headquarters of the Ogden Police Department. Explaining that the depot was closed and my train wouldn't arrive for hours, I asked the desk sergeant for permission to get out of the cold by waiting in the lobby, which was open all night. He refused.

Everyplace else was buttoned up for the night, so the only option was to wait for the train in an open-air shelter beside the locked depot. By the time the train arrived in the wee hours, my fingernails were blue. My next column upon returning home was about flirting with hypothermia, courtesy of the Ogden Police Department. A few days later, Ogden's mayor called a press conference to give me hell for it.

Happily, other destinations the paper chose to send me were both friendlier and more interesting. As touched upon in an earlier chapter, Sports Editor Jim Poore charmed the bosses into sending him and me to the Soviet Union for no clearer objective than to write about, in his words, "what life is like there."

The only way to go to the Soviet Union at that time was to book a tour through Intourist, the official government tourist agency. Jim and I were joined by Boiseans Duane and Lori Stueckle. Our group had guides for both the Moscow and Leningrad portions of the tour, but there was enough free time to do some exploring on our own. An indelible memory is of spending some time chatting with a group of twenty-somethings on a bridge in Moscow. They were as eager to practice their English as we were to pepper them with questions about their country and their lives.

"See these flags?" one of them said, pointing to red cardboard pennants used to decorate the bridge.

"Yes. What about them?"

"One of our friends is in prison for stealing one of them."

"In prison for stealing a cardboard flag? You're kidding!"

"No. He was sentenced to seven years."

The night we left Moscow for Leningrad, now known again by its pre-Soviet name of Saint Petersburg, two men abruptly pulled our tour guide off of the train. We had become quite fond of Natasha, whom we'd gotten to know fairly well during our time in Moscow. She was in tears the last time we saw her as the train left the station. Natasha was replaced by another guide, no explanation given.

Breakfast virtually every morning of the tour was fried eggs, cooked so little that the whites were mostly clear. In our room at the high-rise Intourist Hotel, the walls didn't meet in the corners of the shower, allowing water to drain to God knew where. We were one of the first tour groups to stay in a new, luxury hotel in the village of Suzdal. It was built of beautiful marble, but the marble blocks of the ground floor were sinking, turning the lobby floor into an obstacle course.

One Russian we interviewed concluded our conversation by saying "you more happy than we."

We probably were. And we were undeniably happy to have the freedom to leave, a luxury denied to all but the most-privileged Soviet citizens.

Traveling the country by rail was a joy, Ogden notwithstanding. Traveling to England and Russia with Jim and the Stueckles was delightful. Traveling to Albania was something else.

The Statesman sent photographer Gerry Melendez and me to Albania during the 1999 Kosovo War. I agreed to go because it was a rare opportunity, but it would be dishonest not to admit to some misgivings. Albania under Stalinist dictator Enver Hoxcha was one of the most isolated and repressive countries on the planet. It was the world's first officially atheist state. Religion was outlawed, religious leaders executed. Hoxha presided over mass imprisonments and bloody purges. Under his rule, Albania was cordoned off from the rest of the world for four decades, with few allowed to enter or leave the country. I'd read so many horror stories about Albania through the years that the prospect of going there made me as nervous as I'd ever been.

Gerry and I ostensibly were going there to report on Idahoans involved in the war effort. We did some of that, but the stories of Albanians displaced by the war were far more compelling.

The Statesman arranged for us to hitch a ride as far as England on a KC-135 Stratotanker from Mountain Home Air Force Base. The pilots let us visit with them in the cockpit, and a crew member showed us how to operate the refueling boom by lying in a glass bubble in the belly of the plane, operating a control stick similar to those used in video games. We spent several days at a Royal Air Force base in England before taking a train to London for our flights to Bologna, Italy, and from there to Albania.

The Albanian Airlines plane that took us from Bologna to Tirana, Albania's capital, did not inspire confidence. It had what appeared to be duct tape—I am not making this up—affixed to parts of its fuselage like oversized Band-Aids. It was a two-engine propeller plane that held maybe thirty passengers. Gerry and I were the only ones who weren't smoking. The weather outside was sunny, but inside the cabin it was pea-soup fog.

We knew we'd be on the edge of a war zone, but the tanks lining the runway and the profusion of armed soldiers inside the airport were sobering nevertheless. We were beyond relieved to see a couple holding signs with our names on them. *The Statesman* had arranged for Tim and Miranda Penn, former Boiseans living in Tirana, to be our hosts.

It was immediately apparent, to borrow from *The Wizard of Oz*, that we weren't in Kansas any more. Trash a foot or more deep lined Tirana's streets. Almost everyone drove beat-up Mercedes Benz automobiles, not for their luxury features but because they were the only cars durable enough to hold up on Albania's primitive roads. The drain in the Penns' shower doubled as a toilet.

The war was fought by Albanians against Yugoslavian, primarily Serbian, persecution of Kosovo Albanians. Our second-best story from Albania was about a teacher who started a school in a refugee camp and was teaching Albanian children the heritage they were forbidden from learning when Serbia controlled Kosovo. We spent a long day in the camp, interviewing and photographing the teacher and students. It was late that night by the time we finished sending the story and photos to *The Statesman*. We were exhausted but happy, knowing we'd done good work and had filed a thought-provoking story.

It never ran. We didn't know that until we returned to Boise and failed to find it in back issues or in the *Statesman* archives. An editor who had read it sheepishly told us it had gotten lost. Never before or since had one of my stories been "lost."

The other story we filed that day was not lost. It was one on which we had spent at most half an hour: a few paragraphs and a photo of a tight-lipped Boise woman who had arrived in Tirana to do volunteer work and refused to give us more than two minutes of her time. I asked her a few quick questions; Gerry took a "mug shot" of her. A nothing story that not only was not lost but ran prominently on the front page.

Upon returning home, we learned that *The Statesman*'s editor had titled our series of stories "Idahoans in Service." We could not imagine a more restrictive title. It rendered our best work, stories about Albanians whose lives were upended by the war, all but unusable.

Most of our time in Albania was spent in refugee camps, where hundreds of people who had lost their homes lived cheek to jowl in tents. These were people who had lost not only their homes but their livelihoods—many were professional people—and in more than a few cases their loved ones. The sadness was palpable. I'll never forget being in a camp when (and what are the odds of this?) the inimitable voice of Nat King Cole on a portable radio drifted through the tent city on the evening air.

Smile, though your heart is aching.
Smile even though it's breaking.
You'll find that life is still worthwhile,
If you'll just smile.

At once comforting and heartbreaking.

Our best story from the trip was about a group of women and girls living in a refugee camp. Our conversation with the camp's administrator one evening was abruptly interrupted by unearthly wailing and shrieking. It literally gave us goosebumps. Neither of us had ever heard anything like it.

"What in God's name is that?"

The administrator explained that the source of the sound was a group of some forty Albanian women and girls who gathered under a tree each evening to mourn the loss of their men. Serbian soldiers had come to their village and killed almost every last man: their fathers, brothers, husbands, sons, grandsons, boyfriends. Only a single male survived, by lying face down among the bodies and pretending to be dead.

It was one of those stories you're reluctant to do out of respect for the victims' grief and privacy, but too compelling a story not to do. We anxiously approached the women and asked through an interpreter whether they would be willing to talk to us. Expecting to be rebuffed, we were welcomed. The women and girls were not only willing but eager to tell their story. They wanted the world to know about their loss, their anguish, the atrocities committed against their people.

We left the camp in silence. Their stories of almost unimaginable cruelty and suffering left us too drained to talk about them.

It was the wee hours of the next morning when we filed our story and photos. A framed copy of one of Gerry's photos, a portrait shot of a young girl with her fingers pressed to her mouth and a tear running down her cheek, graces my home office to this day.

"God, Tim!" Gerry said when he finished reading my story on his laptop. "This is the best thing you've ever done."

As published, it was unrecognizable. In her effort to make our stories conform to her "Idahoans in Service" label, the executive editor had much of it cut and interspersed what remained with wire-service copy about Idahoans in the war zone. The best story I ever wrote, in my opinion as well as Gerry's, became an almost unreadable mishmash of factoids that had little or nothing to do with one another. Gerry's beautiful photo, the one so moving that it remains on my wall more than twenty years later, was never published.

He was so angry when he saw what happened to the stories we'd worked so hard on—eighteen-hour days were frequent in Albania—that he vowed to quit and soon did. A gifted photographer and one of the nicest people I ever worked with, Gerry left *The Statesman* within a few months and has spent the rest of his career as an award-winning photojournalist and filmmaker in South Carolina.

Though just as angry as he was, I had little choice but to stick it out at *The Statesman*. Boise was my lifelong home. I'd been at *The Statesman* almost thirty years and in all likelihood was too old to land a job somewhere else.

So I stayed. But when I look at Gerry's powerful photo on my wall and think about the best story I ever wrote that the readers never got to read, it still raises my blood pressure.

CHAPTER ELEVEN
Love Affair with Idaho

All of us wonder about the decisions that shape our lives. Would they have been better if we'd lived somewhere else, made different friends, married a different person?

I sometimes wonder how my life would have been different if I'd followed my father's advice and become a lawyer or a doctor, taken a job offer from *The Seattle Times* early in my career or, as some of my former colleagues did, given up journalism for public relations.

I certainly would have made more money. When I retired after forty years, I was making a little over $70,000 a year. Deciding to become a journalist was never about money, though. It was about doing what I thought I'd be good at and would love.

And my love affair with Idaho grew each year.

An editor once half-joked that there was no corner of the state I hadn't trod. It was an exaggeration, but not by much. My job took me from Bear Lake, in the southeast corner of Idaho, to West Yellowstone (northeast corner) to the Duck Valley Indian Reservation (southwest corner) to Good Grief (far north, near the Canadian border).

At Bear Lake, I made the mistake of trying to drive to the lake's edge and got my car stuck, up to the middle of its wheels in the beach's soft sand. It was late fall, with virtually no one around. If a friendly gent in a Jeep with a winch and a tow cable hadn't happened by, who knows how long I could have been stuck there?

At West Yellowstone, I was honored to cover the Nez Perce Tribe's first buffalo hunt in generations—young boys learning their tribe's heritage by doing what their ancestors had done out of necessity.

At Duck Valley, I covered the wedding of two septuagenarians, one of them the beloved postmaster of Bruneau, Idaho. (I had met Fern Graham years earlier when, in her haste to get the mail out on time, she tugged from the other side of the wall on an envelope I was pushing into a mail slot).

Intrigued by bumper stickers reading "Where the hell is Good Grief, Idaho?"—a place I'd never heard of—I drove more than 400 miles to see where and what it was. (A pizza parlor, and not much else.)

In 1977, when Governor Cecil Andrus was named President Jimmy Carter's Interior Secretary and Lieutenant Governor John Evans became governor, *The Statesman* sent me to Evans's hometown of Malad City to do a story about him. Though Evans had served as lieutenant governor and in the state legislature, he had largely been eclipsed by the popular and charismatic Andrus and was relatively unknown to many Idahoans. I spent several days in Malad City interviewing people who knew him as a way of introducing him to readers who didn't. The locals universally seemed to like and admire him, and time would affirm their opinion of him. Evans served the duration of Andrus's term and was elected twice in his own right, one of only two Democratic governors elected in Idaho in my lifetime. He was a good governor and a genuinely nice man. He was never too busy to answer a question, grant an interview, or chat with ordinary folks. When I wrote a column he especially liked, he sent me a copy of it with a handwritten message, laminated and bearing his signature and the state seal.

Two things surprised me about Malad City. One was that despite being minutes from the Utah border and overwhelmingly Mormon, it had bars that were crowded every night. The other was that the church on the hill prominently overlooking the town was Protestant rather than LDS. A service was held there once a month by a minister who ruefully told me that he was "the loneliest man in town."

Idaho's natural beauty never failed to impress. Time and again while driving its freeways, state highways, and back roads, I was struck by how diverse the state is, how it delights the senses in so many different ways. You can stand on a mountainside and see nothing but snowy peaks in every direction all the way to the horizon. You can go for a day's drive and enjoy the beauty of a mountain stream, an alpine lake, and a jaw-dropping canyon. You can get out of your car on a desert highway and smell the sage, hear only the wind, see nothing that isn't natural.

Upper Mesa Falls, a natural wonder unknown even to many Idahoans, is one of the more spectacular sights anywhere in the country. Blessedly remote, reached only by walking a steep trail from a highway a mere twelve miles long through a forested corner of northeast Idaho, it is unspoiled, majestic, heart-stoppingly beautiful. Unlike Niagara and other well-known waterfalls with crowds of tourists, it seems almost primeval—just the ancient forest, the timeless river, and the solitary spectacle of the falls. You can go there and not see another soul.

A young Wallace Stegner stood beside "the falling tons of water" and watched it "thunder into foam, smooth to green glass over sunken rocks, shatter to foam again. I was fascinated by how it sped by and yet was always there; its roar shook both the earth and me.

"… By such a river it is impossible to believe that one will ever be tired or old. Every sense applauds it. Taste it, feel its chill on the teeth: It is purity absolute." [1]

A plan to develop the falls for hydropower thankfully came to nothing. Upper Mesa Falls should remain pristine. It doesn't need to be "improved" by little men with big, bad ideas. It's perfect just as it is.

Time permitting when a story idea took me to eastern Idaho, I avoided the interstate that crosses the southern part of the state from Oregon to Utah. The interstate will show you pavement, exit signs, distant vistas, and not much else. Infinitely preferable, to my way of thinking, is U.S. Highway 20, which never failed to delight the eyes and lift my spirits.

Drive U.S. 20. It's well worth your time. No other highway shows the diversity of Idaho to better advantage. Leaving the Interstate east of Mountain Home, you climb through rugged hills, pass a reservoir and a cottonwood glade, and climb again to the rolling Camas Prairie. Near Hill City, you pass the draw where Sunrise lived in his covered wagon and a few miles later come to Corral, where Bob Ertter, "the prairie captain" with the double life, made his home. If your timing is right in the spring, you'll pass mile after mile of the lavender Camas flowers that give the prairie its name.

A turn to the north onto Highway 75 will take you to Sun Valley, America's first ski resort. No place else is quite like Sun Valley. Its hills and mountains, some forested, some nearly treeless, look like no hills or mountains anywhere else in the state. Sun Valley is beautiful in any season—snow-covered and reminiscent of an Austrian village in winter, its hills dotted with yellow aspen groves in the fall, green and lovely in spring and summer. My earliest memories of it are of going there with my mother and sister as a young boy, when condominiums were yet to be invented and it truly was a village. We amused ourselves by counting the out-of-state license plates in the lodge parking lot. When we were in junior high, a friend's parents took me with them for a Sun Valley vacation. In Ketchum, a mile from the Sun Valley Resort, we met actress Ann Sothern, who at the time was the star of a hit television series. Lucille Ball, no slouch at comedy herself, called Sothern "the best comedian in the business, bar none." My friend and I met her at a sewing shop she owned. We were starstruck, but she quickly put us at ease, chatting with us like a friendly aunt. She let us sit on the red seats of her white Ford Thunderbird convertible.

Continuing east instead of turning north to Sun Valley, Highway 20 takes you to Picabo, briefly famous for an Olympic skier, Picabo Street, who hailed from there. The most interesting thing about Picabo the town, however, is its general store. Nowhere else in Idaho will you find such a variety of items for sale in a such a small building. You can buy anything from a sledgehammer to lingerie there, and grab a sandwich at its lunch counter. I asked its owner once if there was anything the store didn't sell. After a long pause to ruminate on it, he replied, "Yes. We don't sell cars. … But we used to."

Six miles up the highway from Picabo is Carey, a comparative metropolis with a population of just under a thousand. There once was a house just south of Carey that must have had thirty or forty DeSotos parked outside. DeSotos were my favorite cars during my kid days, and I desperately wanted to interview the owner to do a story about the collection. I must have stopped and knocked on the door half a dozen time through the years, but there was never anyone at home.

Carey was home to late Idaho Secretary of State Pete Cenarrusa, the longest-serving secretary of state in the U.S. Formerly a state legislator, he remains the longest-serving elected official in Idaho's history. What many didn't know about the state official they invariably saw in a suit and tie was that he was also a sheep rancher. Hoping to capture that side of him, I spent a day touring his ranch on foot and in his pickup truck, listening to country music and hearing stories about sheep herding and his Basque heritage. He was dressed that day in jeans, a Western shirt, and a cowboy hat. It was a day well and enjoyably spent with one of the most affable men ever to hold a state office.

A short drive from Carey takes the traveler to Craters of the Moon National Monument, an other-worldly expanse of lava flows and cinder cones. The resemblance to the lunar surface was considered close enough that Apollo 14 astronauts trained there. From there to Idaho Falls, you pass through a stretch of desert some would call desolate but I've always found beautiful. There's something about all that wide open space, the desert wind, and the enveloping silence, that opens the mind and perhaps the soul. The wind comes from so far and goes so far, to places only imagined. I never fail to stop there, to get out of the car, to look and listen, and feel better about the world.

Next stop, Arco: home of the Idaho Nuclear Laboratory and formerly the home of the late Charles "Fuzzy" Steuart. Steuart was a brilliant doctor—manga cum laude Harvard and Johns Hopkins, a founder of Boise's Mountain States Tumor Institute, a physician liked and admired by virtually everyone who knew him. Weary of the medical bureaucracy, he retired and moved to Arco, where he saw patients on his front porch and charged $10 for an appointment. If you didn't have $10, he'd barter with you. He said he called himself Fuzzy instead of Charles because with a name like Fuzzy it's difficult to take yourself too seriously.

From Idaho Falls, the highway turns north and climbs through Ashton and the meadows, grasslands, and forest of Island Park, crosses the Continental Divide, and enters Montana just west of Yellowstone Park. If there are prettier, more interesting roads in Idaho, I haven't traveled them.

The road wasn't the only place where I met unforgettable characters. Some of those I worked with became lifelong friends.

At a press club New Year's Eve party during my first year at *The Statesman*, I was accosted by a man who spun me around, briefly inspected me and without so much as a hello exclaimed, "You don't have blue eyes!"

That was my introduction to John Collias, an artist who had done watercolor portraits used as conversation pieces for the party. He'd painted mine from a black-and-white photo and given it blue eyes. John was well known as the artist who did pen-and-ink portraits for a weekly *Statesman* feature and for artwork that was ubiquitous in Boise, from oil paintings gracing living rooms, corporate headquarters, and the governor's office to the Bronco on the basketball court and blue football field at Boise State University. Raised in Fort Wayne, Indiana, where his parents ran a restaurant and pool hall, he was Greek American to the bone, spoke Greek fluently, and had the fiery temperament and zest for life characteristic of many Greeks. There was no such thing as a boring conversation with John. We enjoyed countless lunches together at Marie's La Fiesta Restaurant, now a memory, from literally the beginning of my career to the end and beyond. Despite being a generation older, he was one of my best friends. He remained so until his death at ninety-eight.

Looking back, it isn't surprising that three of my best friends from work were artists rather than journalists. I've always been more comfortable in the company of artists and musicians. In addition to John, my other artist friends were graphic artist Grady Meyers and sculptor-painter Ann LaRose. Both worked as illustrators in the newsroom. Grady, a gentle giant and Vietnam War veteran with a penchant for old cars (he drove a 1958 Chrysler Imperial and a three-wheeled, wooden Morgan) was one of the funniest people I've ever known. Ann is one of most talented. Her sculptures grace public buildings and private homes throughout the United States.

The most unlikely friendship from my newspaper career was with a circus promoter. Bill Kay was the producer of the El Korah Shrine Circus, which came to town every June for three decades. He was a big man who adored good food, dressed in cheap suits and a Shriner's fez, and was a larger-than-life figure whose stories mesmerized anyone within earshot. When he arrived each summer with news releases about the circus, anyone who wasn't racing a deadline gathered round to hear his tales of circus life, eateries he'd discovered in his travels, and whatever else sprang from his prolific well of stories. He'd dined at the Waldorf Astoria, been gored by an elephant, traveled with the legendary Spike Jones on his private railroad train. He sent me menus from restaurants that impressed him and on one occasion shipped me a seafood dinner from the Gulf Coast, packed in dry ice.

If I had to name the best things about my career as a journalist, friendships would be high on the list. Others would be the hundreds if not thousands of fascinating people I was fortunate to interview and write about, the places I was privileged to visit and of course the work itself. I love to write. Nothing makes me happy in the same way as finishing a good piece. To be able to do that and get paid for it seems almost too good to be true. When you think of all the people who hate their jobs, the good fortune of having one you love is priceless.

If I'm completely honest, I have to admit to being a bit disappointed at not having become the novelist my adolescent self pictured when I was certain that I'd be the next John Steinbeck. I lacked an important quality for that, a novelist's imagination. The process by which novelists imagine one engaging plot after another, some authors coming up with enough of them to write scores of books, remains a wonder to me.

Things didn't work out badly, though. I would be remiss in identifying the good things about my career not to include the readers. Letters and emails received from them numbered in the thousands. Some were negative, and a comparatively high percentage of those made their way to the editorial page. If people like what you write, they tell you personally or send you a letter or an email. If they don't like something you write, they write a scathing letter to the editor. The great majority of letters, emails, and personal encounters, however, were positive, and many were heartwarming. I'm grateful for every one of them.

As much as it meant to me, I didn't fully appreciate the connection with the readers until I retired from *The Statesman*. I told Vicki Gowler, then the executive editor, that I didn't want to make a big deal of it, adding that I'd just as soon pass on a newsroom sendoff with a cake and gifts.

"No," she replied. "We have to make a big deal of it."

The newsroom sendoff included personal friends, former coworkers, a speech by former Governor and Interior Secretary Dirk Kempthorne and, to my surprise, an impromptu performance by the Mystics. The guys had sneaked some guitars, a couple of small amplifiers and a mini-drum kit into the newsroom when my back was turned.

Vicki and Publisher Mi-Ai Parrish also arranged a public reception in the city's largest park. Expecting perhaps thirty or forty people, I was blown away by a crowd of hundreds—Secretary of State Pete Cenarrusa, Paul and Sydney Revere, former editors and fellow reporters, people I'd written about … But primarily readers, people who said they'd read my work and wanted to say thanks. Some had driven hours from other parts of the state to be there. Many wanted me to sign books or yellowed clippings of stories that had meant something to them. Both gratifying and humbling, it was one of the best days of my life. I was touched beyond words.

Sometimes I envy people who from a young age know exactly what they want to do with their lives and methodically set about achieving it. I had no such vision or sense of purpose. My life was never planned. It was always a take-things-as-they-come and try to make the best of them sort of thing. I never did become the highly paid professional my father envisioned or the novelist I pictured in in my youthful imaginings; I just more or less drifted with the tide from one thing to the next.

And more often than not, got lucky. I married a good woman, have three great kids, and did work that was fulfilling, sometimes thrilling, and almost never boring.

The decision made at my father's desk so many years ago, to pursue a career doing what I loved rather than something that paid big bucks, paid dividends worth far more than money.

It would have been nice if my parents had lived to attend the retirement party in the park. Dad would have realized that even though I never performed a surgery or wrote a legal brief, things turned out okay.

Actually, he seemed to have known that for some time. Among his belongings that we found after he died was a stack of clippings—dozens of my old columns, carefully tied together with a length of ribbon.

Mom? She'd have been happy that her stick-to-it-ivness lectures had had an effect.

"I'm proud of you," she'd have said had she been there on that day in the park. "But be sure to stand up straight and not slouch. And you should have worn a tie. There are a lot of people here, and it's important to make a good impression."

[1] *Cort Conley, "Idaho for the Curious," Backeddy Books, 278*

AFTERWORD

Ten years have passed since that day in the park. More than a few times since then, I've been reminded of a remark by a typesetter named Dar Peterson. I happened to run into Dar not long after he retired and asked him how he was doing.

"When you retire," he replied, "you'll wonder how you ever had time to work."

A career may end, but the days continue to be filled. Mine have been as busy in retirement as they were before.

I'd been retired for three months when Sheila and I were invited to a dinner party. One of the guests who happened to be on the board of a homeless shelter suggested that I might enjoy volunteering there. That was the beginning of a nine-year stint of volunteering every other Tuesday morning. The nine years ended with the beginning of the Covid-19 pandemic and the shelter's management deeming it too risky for elderly volunteers to continue. I still have trouble thinking of myself as elderly, but there you are,

It was nice not to have column deadlines any more, but after a few months of puttering around the house and taking a couple of trips I missed doing the column and inquired about writing as a freelancer. The result was a column every other Sunday. A nice retirement pace.

My relationship with *The Statesman* ended after a new editor cut the frequency of my columns and restricted me to writing only about "people in the community." When she changed the name of the column from the "Tim Woodward" column to the "Community Focus" column, I quit and started writing for *The Idaho Press*.

As of this writing, I've been doing that for three years. Working with people at *The Press* has been a joy.

The Mystics continue to play and in my opinion are getting better with age. The only nonprofessional musician in the group, I'm fortunate to be working with gifted professionals. Playing with the Mystics has been one of the most enjoyable things in my life.

Sheila retired from her career as an elementary school teacher a year before I retired and continues to outdo herself as a grandmother extraordinaire and one of the most thoughtful, generous people I know. Our daughter Andie is a flight paramedic. Jennifer, our younger daughter, is a registered nurse. Our son, Mark, works for a company that makes ergonomic furniture. Grandchildren Hailey, Kelsie, Ryan, and Chloe, and great-grandson Grayson, all live in Boise and are important parts of our lives.

Not long before I retired, I got a call that almost led to a new career. It was from actor George Kennedy, who had left Hollywood for a quieter lifestyle in Idaho. He said he wanted to make a television series about some of the colorful characters I'd written about for my columns and feature stories. He envisioned it as being similar to the late Charles Kuralt's *On the Road* series. George would be the host. He'd do the show's introductions; I'd interview the subjects and write the scripts. A Boise company, Wide Eye Productions, would do the filming.

We were so close! We filmed a pilot segment, had two cable networks and a hotel-chain sponsor ready to commit and were planning to go national. That would have meant a lot of traveling, meaning I'd have to quit my newspaper job. It all ended when George, for reasons we were never certain of, backed out of doing the show. Without the celebrity host, there was no show. My guess is that when he understood the time commitment that would be involved, he got cold feet.

Things worked out, though. George and I hit it off and became pals. He loved going to obscure restaurants, little-known gems in out-of-the-way places, and we enjoyed numerous breakfasts, lunches, and dinners together. I never tired of listening to his tales of working with Cary Grant, Audrey Hepburn, Clint Eastwood, Jimmy Stewart, Paul Newman, and other stars.

Though the loss of the show was disappointing to all involved, with the probable exception of George, the failed project led to one that made up for it. Instead of a Charles Kuralt-type television show, Wide Eye Productions opted to make a film about Idaho. I wrote the scripts and did the narration. *Idaho, the Movie* DVDs sold in every state and some forty foreign countries. It won Emmy and Telly awards, is viewed regularly on Amazon Prime and recently was approved for worldwide streaming.

In 2016, Sheila and I went to Africa. We're sponsors of two students at Boisean Vincent Kituku's Caring Hearts and Hands of Hope High School in Kenya, and the trip was our chance to visit the school and meet them. On our way home, we extended our layover in Europe and visited my old Navy haunts in Bremerhaven. The city had changed so much I barely recognized it. Its charming, Old World downtown had become a mall. The base where my fellow sailors and I spied on the East German, Polish, and Russian navies is now a housing development and medical center.

The last two years have been dominated by the Covid-19 pandemic. We've spent much of that time at home, leaving only when necessary. Getting vaccinated gave us freedoms we'd almost forgotten, but with new variants of the virus emerging I'm spending as much or more time than ever at home—reading and writing, practicing on my guitars, puttering in the house and yard, walking the dog. In my twilight years, more demanding things I once enjoyed no longer interest me as much. One of life's hardest lessons is how quickly it passes.

It's easier to accept if it's been a fulfilling life, though, and in that I've been lucky. Lucky to have grown up in such an idyllic place and to have spent much of my time doing what I loved: reading, writing, and playing music.

Old and creaky as I'm getting, I can't sit still very long and don't do well with too much leisure. Now that this book is finished, I'll need another project.

A book of profiles about the colorful Idaho characters I've interviewed?

A novel, perhaps?

With apologies to John Steinbeck, maybe it's not too late.

ACKNOWLEDGMENTS

Thanks to Pat Carson for proofreading the manuscript and giving me her impressions and sound advice. Thanks to Cort Conley for encouraging me to write a memoir, proofreading the manuscript and helping me decide on a title. Thanks to Jeanne Huff for editing the book and my columns for *The Idaho Press* and for being a steadfast advocate. Without her and *Idaho Press* Publisher Matt Davison, this book would not have been published. And thanks, as ever, to my family for putting up with the ups and downs of living with a journalist and musician.